BLACK & Magic PURPLE Passion

Written and Published
by
KAREN PLATT

British Library Cataloguing in publication data.
A catalogue record of this book is available from the British Library.

ISBN 0- 9528810-55

Website www.seedsearch.demon.co.uk
e-mail k@seedsearch.demon.co.uk

First published in Great Britain 2000 by Karen Platt.

Photographs
Front Cover: Aquilegia 'William Guiness', Helleborus orientalis hybrid, Dianthus barbatus 'Sooty'.
Photo Credits: Ray Brown, Plantworld. Devon.
Back Cover: Dracunculus vulgaris, Hydrangea, Iris chrysographes.
Photo Credits: Ray Brown, Plantworld. Devon.
Inside Front Cover: Dianthus Black and White Minstrels Group. Photo Credit: Thompson & Morgan, Ipswich.

This book is dedicated to all those people and things which became a passion.

CONTENTS

INTRODUCTION

The ideas in this book stem from the time I first became professionally involved with gardening. It had long been a hobby and on giving up teaching, I had more time to devote to my garden.

I became fascinated by 'black' plants and the first ones to catch my eye were amazingly black. Ophiopogon planiscapus 'Nigrescens' infected me hopelessly, and I was further smitten by Iris chrysographes and the 'black' Primula auriculas. I started to deliberately seek out more 'black' plants and the fever has continued and become a passion which I know will never cease. My passion led to the creation of what must have been the smallest nursery in the world, set up in my back garden. I grew everything I sold on my own, I did not buy in any stock and much of what I sold was seed-raised. I learned by trial and error and enjoyed myself immensely. The seed-raising led to quite a different adventure, when I launched the book, The Seed Search to let everyone know the wealth of plants which can be raised from seed. At the same time, I moved house and I lost my little nursery. That is the time I conceived the idea of writing about black plants, if I no longer had the space to grow them lovingly, I could at least let others know what is available. My idea for a book on black and white plants was turned down by Frances Lincoln publishers, so I put it on the back boiler and gathered information until the time was right financially for me to publish the book myself.

That time has been used wisely. There are now far more 'black' plants around than there were almost four years ago and I feel I am able to offer so much more. So much information is here that I thought it would detract somewhat from the 'black' plants

if I also included white plants, so it has become a book exclusively of dark plants.

'Black' plants are sexy, mysterious, fashionable, exciting and ultimately desirable not sombre, menacing or funereal. The little black dress has long been the garb of the sophisticated lady. Black is the colour of the sophisticated, modern garden.

Purple is regal and passionate and has just been voted the colour of the new Millenium. For me it is a wide colour range and I prefer to choose bronzy-purple or purple-black which is ideally suited to the dark garden. Deepest, darkest violet flowers can also be very attractive.

I believe dark plants deserve a place in every garden, even if only as accent plants, although it is now possible to create a completely dark garden or corner of the garden. They combine well with other colours. Dark foliage plants often have perfectly contrasting flowers of white, pink, blazing red, bright yellow or orange. They also associate well with silvery foliage. Foliage comes in all shapes, sizes and textures so you cannot be at a loss to create an interesting border, or other plantings, such as for the pondside. There are also numerous tender plants which can be used for summer bedding. The 'black' interest can be extended with black berries which can persist into winter.

I hope you will catch some of my enthusiasm for these wonderful plants, descriptions are first-hand or I have acknowledged nurseries where they have given descriptions. I do not just like 'black' plants, I adore them and feel an overwhelming passion for them. I would choose a black plant time and time again before choosing any other colour.

I hope you will enjoy this book as much as I have writing it.

Karen Platt.   February 2000.

4

IN THE PAST AND THE PRESENT

'Black' plants are considered to be the most elusive of plants, and in the past they have commanded enormous sums of money. Testifying to their popularity in the past is the Garden Book by Sir Thomas Hamner which was completed in 1659, but not published until 1933, in which he describes the ever-increasing colour range of Auriculas in the mid seventeenth century. He was successful in raising many new varieties including one which he named 'Black Imperial' - the darker the flower the more desirable it was.

In 1756, Count Grigorijj Demidov, the owner of gardens in Western Siberia, sent to Peter Collinson a lily 'as near to black as any flower'.

A certain Flora nigra, reputed to be black was offered at £21 in the catalogue of one Robert Edmeades in 1776. Black Primula auriculas were also on offer as well as Ranunculus in combinations of black and coffee, black and violet, black-brown and dark olive.

Black has always been the most sought after and favoured colour in flowers from Tulips to the elusive black Rose. Redoute mentioned dark roses in his book. Rosa rubrifolia with its wine-coloured foliage, particularly beneath. Rosa pimpinellifolia Mariaeburgensis with its black hips. Rosa gallica purpurea velutina parva which he also noted as being called 'Van Eeden's Rose' and describes as having brilliant purple flowers, on opening an admirable violet, velvety look. The petals finally blacken before falling and thereby offer the elusive 'black rose'. Rosa gallica purpureoviolacea magna, 'Bishop's Rose' is featured as a fine purple-violet flowered form with reddish stems. Rosa gallica mahaka flore subsimplici 'Near single Maheka', also known as 'The Fair Sultana' is a magnificent gallica with very deep dark red velvet flowers and Rosa gallica gueriniana , 'Guerin's Rose' which is a fine violet is also described.

Nowadays, there are breeding programmes to produce dark foliage and flowers and some recent advances have been made with regard to several species. There are many dark foliaged hardy Geraniums and Heucheras to choose from and many named Iris hybrids and Primula auricula with dark flowers. Ever more species are coming to the fore with darker flowers such as Agapanthus and Dierama.

COLOUR

Very few plants are truly black in colour. The nearest to black foliage plant is Ophiopogon planiscapus 'Nigrescens' and the nearest to black flowers are found in Iris chrysographes and Fritillaria camschatcensis.

So what is it that makes black plants so special? I think partly it is their elusive quality but also a truly black or near black plant is of such exquisite and unusual beauty that it cannot go unnoticed. The colour can be affected by several factors.

Colour is subjective and what one person calls plum purple could be described differently by half a dozen others. Colour is also affected by the amount of light upon it. Dark plants usually colour best in full sun, although dark flowers on Hemerocallis will fade in full sun. The glaucous purple foliage of Rosa glauca is attractive in full sun, in shade it looks greyish-green with a mauve tinge. This is applicable to many dark foliage plants whose green tones will show through in shade. Bear this is mind when you are buying a dark foliage plant, if you are attracted to it because of its glowing foliage and it is growing in full sun, plant it up in the same position in your garden to achieve the same effect. Even feeding the plant correctly or incorrectly can affect the colouring as well as the soil in which it is grown. Juxtaposition also affects how dark plants look. Planted with white Tulips the plum purple of T.'Queen of Night' will look darker. It is the contrast which enhances the darker colour.

'Black' flowers appear to fall into categories which include other tones such as black-blue, black-purple, black-maroon, dark foliage is purple, black-purple, purple-bronze, black-green or purple-green. I have a bias towards the darkest foliage and the black-maroon category of flowers, although naturally I prefer pure black in both when available. Curiously, dark flowers and foliage rarely come together, but can be found in Dianthus barbatus 'Sooty'.

There is little indication of the darkness of flower or foliage from either common or latin names. A plant bearing the word 'Black' in its cultivar name, is not necessarily so.

The specific epithets indicating black or blackish in the botanical name such as niger, nigra, nigrescens, nigricans are no indication either of black flowers or foliage. In many cases they refer to other parts of the plant, such as in Juglans nigra which refers to the dark bark or as in Helleborus niger which refers to the root. To be sure you are getting the colour you want, try to buy in bloom, although this may not always be possible, black plants are often rare and disappear fast, you will often find there is a waiting list for some of these beauties, but then you will always find them worth the wait.

USING THE BOOK

Plants listed in alphabetical order in the main section are the key black plants, although some of them you may wish to reject as not dark enough for your dark garden, depending on how strict you wish to be. In this section, I have tried to select plants whose foliage retains its dark colour year-round, but one or two have slipped through my net and for the continuity of the book are included in the main section. In the subsections, there are lists of plants whose foliage emerges dark or turns dark in autumn or winter, but during the rest of the year is not so dark or even entirely green.

I have also included dark-centred flowers and a list of other darkish plants which may be of interest.

Use the descriptions to select your plants. The descriptions are to the best of my knowledge accurate, if a plant named 'Black' is not so in my opinion, I have indicated this in the text. However, it is important to bear in mind that at some stage you may encounter disappointment when seeking 'black' plants for the reasons stated earlier in this introduction. As with all plantings, if you find something is not suitably dark, take it out and replace it with something else.

HARDINESS

The hardiness of each plant is indicated in the text. This refers to the species described ONLY and is no indication as to the hardiness of other species within the genus. Please note that hardiness is affected by position in the garden and other factors.

SUPPLIERS

When writing to suppliers, PLEASE make sure you send at least a S.A.E. with enquiries. Some nurseries understandably charge for catalogues, please check first.

PLANT PROFILES A-Z

ACACIA

Dark-leaved Acacias are not to be found by the dozen. So this species will come as a pleasant surprise, the foliage is not that dark, just flushed purple. Frost tender.

CULTIVATION
Grow in loam-based compost in full light under glass. When in growth, water freely, applying a balanced feed monthly. Reduce watering in winter. Outdoors grow in moderately fertile, neutral to acid soil in a sheltered site in full sun.

PROPAGATION
Sow seed under glass in spring, pre-soak in warm water until swollen. Root semi-ripe cuttings in summer.

A.baileyana 'Purpurea' has fern-like foliage which is flushed purple and violet. It bears cream flowers in dense racemes from winter to spring and is suitable as a conservatory shrub.

ACAENA

Worthy of a mention for their bronzy foliage. It is often thought that the form 'Kupferteppich' is the best selling Acaena because of its bronze foliage, the burrs add interest too. Some Acaenas are invasive, but this one is well-behaved. Fully hardy.

CULTIVATION
Moderately fertile, well-drained soil in sun or partial shade. Suitable for a rock garden.

PROPAGATION
Sow seed in an open frame in autumn. Separate rooted stems or take softwood cuttings in late spring.

A.microphylla forms a carpet of greeny-bronze foliage. Remove rooted stems if the plant is becoming invasive.

A.microphylla 'Kupferteppich' is often sold as Copper Carpet. It is a well-behaved plant with pinnate bronzed leaves and bright red burrs in late summer. A restrained form which is highly suitable for the rock garden. 3cm.

ACALYPHA

This is a rarely seen Pacific spreading shrub with wonderfully coloured foliage. Frost tender.

CULTIVATION
Under glass, grow in loamless compost in full or filtered light. Water freely when in growth, applying a balanced feed monthly during summer. Reduce watering in winter. Pot on or top dress in early spring or autumn. Outdoors, grow in fertile, humus-rich, moist but well-drained soil in full sun for the best colour. Minimum temperature 10°C (50°F).

PROPAGATION
Root softwood cuttings in early spring or semi-ripe cuttings in late summer with bottom heat.

A.wilkesiana is known as Copperleaf, it bears copper-tinted, variegated leaves, wonderful colouring but not suitable for the dark garden. The two cultivars which follow are of more interest but they will not be easy to find in the U.K.

A.wilkesiana 'Macafeeana' bears deep bronze leaves splashed with copper-red.

A.wilkesiana 'Marginata' bears bronze-red leaves edged with cream or pale pink.

ACER

This genus includes around 150 species of evergreen and deciduous trees and shrubs. Most of them make highly suitable specimen plants offering good autumn colour and many are suitable for container growing even in small gardens, be certain to choose a large container. Maples are grown for their stunning foliage. The attractive opposite leaves are usually lobed, but sometimes unlobed, 3-palmate or pinnate. The small, often greenish flowers are insignificant and the winged fruits (those from the common sycamore tree (A.pseudoplatanus) are often referred to as helicopters) will be familiar to all.

CULTIVATION

Sow in fertile, moist but always well-drained soil in full sun or partial shade. The autumn colours will be produced better if grown in neutral to acid soil. Protect from strong winds and mulch roots in temperatures below freezing. Prune to retain a healthy framework in late autumn to midwinter.

PROPAGATION

A mature Acer is quite an expensive though worthwhile plant. Species can be grown from seed for a fraction of the outlay, but seedlings may be variable. Some cultivars will come true, but are more often grafted. Pre-germinated seeds are also available.

A. negundo v violaceum only reaches about half the size of the large wild green A.negundo. It has purplish new shoots and twigs, the male flower tassels are also purplish. The leaf colour matures rather brownish green-purple.

A.palmatum f atropurpureum
The Japanese purple-leaved Maples are well-known and the most popular in gardens. Its compact forms are suitable for most gardens and it makes a good container subject. The dark purple spring foliage gives way to a paler olive-purple in summer followed by deeper scarlet tones in autumn. It comes largely true from seed when you can expect foliage to vary in colour from bright rusty red to dark purple. Grow a number of seedlings and select the deepest colour. The deeply lobed leaves will redden in autumn.This small tree is also a good subject for bonsai.

A.palmatum 'Beni-kagami' has pendent branches and a bushy habit with 5-lobed red-purple leaves which turn bronzy-red in autumn. Height and spread 8m (25ft).
A. palmatum 'Beni-otake' is a dwarfish form with deeply dissected foliage of deep reddish purple.
A.palmatum 'Bloodgood' is a striking cultivar, smaller than 'Beni-kagami' also having deeply cut 5-lobed leaves of a darker red-purple turning red in autumn.
A.palmatum 'Burgundy Lace' with similar colouring is smaller still. It has fringed foliage at the margins.

A.palmatum v dissectum Dissectum Atropurpureum Group
A diminutive lacy foliage tree with red-purple leaves which are deeply divided. Height 2m (6ft), spread 3m (10ft).
A. palmatum v dissectum 'Crimson Queen' has red-purple deeply and finely

divided foliage throughout the summer and is slightly larger than the above. It has fiery autumn tones.

A.palmatum v dissectum 'Dissectum Nigrum' has dark red-purple leaves, silvery beneath when young.

A.palmatum 'Garnet' retains its red-purple colour into autumn.

A.palmatum 'Hessei' is a superb cultivar with dark crimson deeply divided foliage. Ht 5m (15ft), spread 6m (20 ft).

A. palmatum 'Inaba-shidare' (the name could be a synonym) has deeply cut bronzy red leaves with vigorous new growth.

A. palmatum 'Inazuma' is known as the Thunder Maple. It has rich purple red serrated leaves which turn bronzy green in summer, then crimson in autumn.

A.palmatum 'Linearilobum Atropurpureum' has deeply cut red-purple foliage. Ht 5m (15ft), spread 4m. The cultivar **'Osakazuki'** has slightly bronze foliage.

A. palmatum 'Red Dragon' is a cultivar offering very deep purple-red foliage and retains its excellent colouring through to autumn. **'Red Pygmy'** is a dwarf form growing to around 1.5m (5ft) with reddish purple leaves.

A. palmatum 'Shaina' is an upright growing, compact and dense form with bright red new foliage which matures to a deep maroon red.

A. platanoides 'Crimson King' is a stunning cultivar of the slow-growing Norway Maple with deep crimson-purple leaves, maturing slightly darker and having bright red autumn colour. It is more wind-tolerant than other Maples.

Where space is limited **A.platanoides 'Crimson Sentry'** is narrowly upright and has red-purple foliage. Height 12m (40ft), spread 5m (15ft).

A.platanoides 'Faassen's Black' is similar to but darker than 'Crimson King'. The leaves turn up at the margins.

A.platanoides 'Goldsworth Purple' is a lighter shade with wrinkled young leaves. The red leaves of **A.platanoides 'Schwedleri'** turn dark purple green by summer.

A. pseudoplatanus 'Atropurpureum' offers only dark-red purple on the underside of its leaves with the addition of red leaf stalks. 25m (80ft), spread 20m (70ft).

A: rubrum as its name indicates offers red colour, the darkest cultivar is probably **'Schlesingeri'** whose leaves turn a dark red very early in autumn.

Acers can also offer interesting striped or flaky bark, and are then known as the snake-bark maples.

One example is **A.davidii 'Serpentine'** which has strongly contrasting stripes on a deep purplish brown bark, but unfortunately not purple leaves. Autumn foliage offers yellow, orange and dull scarlet.

AECHMEA

Aechmea is a genus of almost 200 rosette-forming bromeliads. Mainly from rainforests, they are used as houseplants in Great Britain where temperatures fall below 10°C (50 °F). They have attractive, arching leaves which are often marked. Spike-like inflorescences with long-lasting flowers and brightly coloured bracts appear in summer and can be followed by fruits.

CULTIVATION

Epiphytic bromeliad compost will suit these plants best. They need bright filtered light in low humidity. Water freely when in growth and apply a low nitrogen fertiliser once a month. Water by filling the central cup.

Outdoors although they can be grown as epiphytes, they are equally happy on the ground in a moist epiphytic or gritty humus-rich soil.

PROPAGATION

Root offsets in early summer. Seed can be obtained for these and other bromeliads.

A. orlandiana is an epiphytic perennial with rosettes of strap-like leaves in mid-green up to 30cm (1 ft) long. These are banded dark purple with purple marginal spines. In summer, red stems bear pyramidal inflorescences to 10cm (4") long with spikes of 4-6 red-bracted, yellowish white flowers which are 2-3 cm long, followed by ovoid pale green fruit. It is a very fascinating plant.

The leaves of **A.weilbachii** are often tinged purple and **A.nudicaulis** and **A. mertensii** have black marginal spines.

A. Foster's Favourite Group has leaves flushed wine-red.

AEONIUM

This genus of mainly perennial succulents are quite well-known, including the 'black' ones described here. Mediterranean plants, they colour best in sun.

The neat rosettes of fleshy leaves look much better when they start to branch.

CULTIVATION

Where temperatures fall below 10°C (50°F) grow under glass using a cactus compost. Water freely during the growing season, allowing the compost to dry out between waterings. Apply a balanced feed every 6 weeks when in growth. Keep dry when dormant.

The plants can be placed outdoors in summer. To grow outdoors, where temperatures permit, choose a site in partial shade in a moderately fertile, well-drained soil.

PROPAGATION

Grow species from seed, or take rosette cuttings in early summer. Allow a callus to form before inserting into sandy cactus cuttings compost in moderate light at 18°C (64°F). Keep barely moist until roots have formed.

A arboreum 'Atropurpureum' is an erect succulent. Its branches bear tight rosettes of spoon-shaped, dark purple-black leaves which turn green in winter.

A.arboreum 'Zwartkop' is one of the most wonderful black plants and one every enthusiast should choose to grow. Its rich purple-black leaves retain their colour year-round. Flowers are yellow and appear in late spring. Reaches 2m height and spread in Morocco, but will be much smaller here in Great Britain and they are quite slow-growing. Use it indoors in winter and out on the patio in summer.

AESCHYNANTHUS

Easy to grow in cultivation, although most are epiphytes in their natural habitat. The very showy, exotic flowers are suitable for a hanging basket.

CULTIVATION

Indoors, grow in peat-based compost in full light, maintaining a humid atmosphere and a minimum temperature of 10°C (50°F). Occasionally mist in summer. Outdoors grow in part shade in a hanging basket or establish as an epiphyte in a tree, where temperatures allow.

A.Black Pagoda Group bears mottled leaves which are green on the surface and purple underneath. The base of the flower is green shading to deep orange at the tips.
A.'Firewheel' bears young silvery foliage, becoming purple-tinged later. Typical lipstick plant flowers.
A.'Purple Star' might also be of interest.

AJUGA

Offering excellent bronzed foliage, Ajugas make eye-catching carpets when they emerge in May-June. Excellent subjects for ground cover in shade, offering interesting leaf colour. They will spread freely in moist soil. A. chamaepitys is one species that will thrive in dry soil. Fully hardy.

CULTIVATION

Ajugas prefer moist soil in partial shade. Leaves can scorch in full sun. A.reptans can thrive in poor soil in full shade.

PROPAGATION

Species can be grown from seed, cultivars do not come true. Germination may be erratic.

Divide plants at any time in moist, shady conditions. Rooted stems can be separated from the parent plant or softwood cuttings can be taken in summer.

A.reptans 'Atropurpurea' gives a good contrast of deep blue flowers to the burnished purple foliage. 20cm (8").
A.reptans 'Burgundy Glow' has silvery green leaves which are suffused a deep wine-red providing a vivid carpet all winter. 15cm (6").
A. reptans 'Catlin's Giant' has tall flower stems up to 30cm (1ft), bearing rich blue flowers to compliment the purplish brown calyces. New rosettes of large glossy bronze-purple or purple-green leaves to 15cm (6") echo the hue.
A. reptans 'Pink Surprise' is a new introduction from Holland. It has two surprises to please us, pink flowers in April which is quite out of the ordinary for Bugles and impressive dark purple foliage.
A. reptans 'Braunherz' offers deep coppery bronze foliage with the usual blue flowers.

AKEBIA

Twining shrubs offering lovely dark flowers and elegant foliage. Hardy.

CULTIVATION

Grow in a good loamy soil, moist but well-drained.

PROPAGATION

Sow fresh seed in a cold-frame.

A.quinata is a semi-evergreen climber with brownish-purple flowers having a spicy scent.
A.trifoliata is a deciduous climber with purple flowers in spring.
The purple fruits are not often produced in the U.K.

ALCEA

Short-lived perennials or biennials, the most commonly grown being A.rosea which produces some remarkable near black flowers to delight the eye. Funnel shaped flowers are borne in summer. Attractive to butterflies and bees, these tall plants can be grown along a wall or in a mixed border. Fully hardy.

CULTIVATION

Grow in well-drained soil, moderately fertile in full sun. They may need staking, especially in exposed sites. To control Hollyhock rust grow as annuals or biennials, not as perennials.

PROPAGATION

Grow from seed, you can select the best 'black' and collect seed to sow for the following year.

A.rosea is an upright perennial producing rounded, roughly hairy light green leaves with shallow lobes.
A.'Arabian Nights' is a form which offers single and double flowers, near black, glistening maroon, with a lighter maroon ring around the centre, yellow anthers. 2m.
A.rosea 'Black Beauty' is very near black, shining and glistening and quite stunning. Yellow anthers. Perhaps the darkest form available. 2m (6ft)
A.rosea 'Nigra' is also remarkable for its single, deep chocolate-maroon flowers with yellow throats in summer. Can be variable, but at its best it is a stunning black, almost oily, with just a slight hint of purplish red as the blooms age. I do not believe A.rosea **'Watchman'** differs significantly. 2m (6ft).

Near black Hollyhocks are also to be found amongst some colour mixtures such as **A. rosea East Coast Hybrids.** At least 2m.

x ALICEARA

A hybrid genus of evergreen epiphytic orchids. Bearing dark flowers of an incredible beauty. Frost tender.

CULTIVATION

Cool-growing orchids. Grow in epiphytic orchid compost in the smallest possible container. Provide high-humidity in summer, with good ventilation in a shaded spot. Water moderately throughout the year, less so in winter. Give a half-strength fertiliser at every third watering.

PROPAGATION

When the plant has overgrown its container, divide.

x Aliceara 'Dark Warrior' is a real beauty, not at all the image its fierce name conjures up. The racemes of flowers borne throughout the year are typically chocolate brown with cream lips spotted with the same hue. Leaves are green, 23cm (9") long, flowers 4cm across and the plant stands 25cm (10") high. A minimum temperature of 12°C (54°F) is required.

ALLIUM

Ornamental onions have very attractive flowers. Fully hardy.

CULTIVATION

Grow in fertile, well-drained soil in full sun. Bulbs should be planted at a depth of 5-10cm (2-4") in autumn.

PROPAGATION

Sow seed in a cold frame when ripe or in spring.

A.atropurpureum is probably the darkest Allium with dense heads of blackish-purple flowers. 75cm (30").

ALOCASIA

Within the genus of Alocasia are around 70 species of large, evergreen, mainly rhizomatous, sometimes tuberous-rooted perennials. Their natural habitat is tropical forest and sunny, usually damp sites by streams and marshes in south and south-east Asia. They have striking large leaves which demand attention. They are arrow-shaped and astonishingly well-marked often with black, dark violet or bronze. The relatively insignificant spathes can be borne at any time of year and are followed by clusters of red or orange fruits. Unfortunately they are frost tender, but they make superb foliage plants.

CULTIVATION

In frost-prone areas grow under glass in filtered light. A mix of bark, sand and loam will provide a suitable growing medium. In growth, provide high humidity and water freely, more moderately in winter. Feed every 2-3 weeks with a balanced fertiliser.
Moist, humus rich soil will suit them outdoors and a position in partial shade.

PROPAGATION

Seed should be obtained ripe and sown immediately.
Rhizomes can be divided or they can be multiplied by separating offsets in spring or summer. Stem cuttings can be rooted in early spring.

A. 'Black Velvet' is a compact plant with rounded blackish-green leaves to 20cm (8") with exotically veloured surfaces emboldened by irridescent creamy white veins.

A.cuprea, the copper Taro, is a rhizomatous perennial with distinct oblong-ovate leaf blades, 45cm (18") long and leaf stalks 60cm (24") long. Upper leaf surfaces are strikingly marked with dark green metallic zones and midribs with copper coloured areas in between, the undersides being distinctly reddish-violet or maroon-purple. Purple spathes are 15cm (6") long. The plant can reach 1m with a slightly shorter spread. Minimum temperature of 16°C (61°F) is necessary.

A.cuprea 'Blackie' is a cultivar to look out for, but can be difficult to overwinter. It grows to around 1m with heart-shaped deep purple-black leaves. An absolute stunner, needing high temperatures and humidity to do well.

A.plumbea produces purple or dark olive-green stems and similarly coloured elegant, polished ovate leaves with the stunning combination of wavy margins, purple veins and metallic purple colouring on the undersides of the leaves. Each leaf blade is a gigantic 1m (approx. 3ft) long and each leaf stalk the same length. White-ivory hood-shaped spathes 15cm (6") long are produced to contrast beautifully with the dark foliage. I.5m (4-5ft). Hardier than A.cuprea and reasonably easy to maintain. An exquisitely handsome plant.

The leaves of A.sanderiana would not disappoint either, being very dark green to near black with a light green margin.

A.wentii (synonym A.discolor) has peltate leaves with bronzy shades.

AMARANTHUS

Amaranthus is a genus of around 60 species of erect or prostrate and spreading annuals or short-lived perennials from differing habitats. Some have deep red or purple leaves. They can be used as accent plants in summer bedding schemes in frost-prone areas. They are half-hardy.

CULTIVATION
Under glass grow in full light. Water freely in summer and provide high humidity. Outdoors they will do well protected from strong winds. Grow in a moderately fertile, humus-rich soil in full sun. Water freely during summer, especially in dry periods to promote flowering. A.caudatus tolerates poor soil.

PROPAGATION
Sow seed indoors or in situ for A.caudatus.

A.caudatus, commonly known as Love-lies-bleeding has many cultivars with purple foliage. Deep red tassel-like pendent flowers are unusual and appear freely from summer to early autumn.

A.cruentus bears purplish green leaves but nothing to compare with the cultivars of the above species.

A.hypochondriacus leaves are heavily suffused with purple. There is a form with leaves so dark-red as to almost appear black. It grows to 1.5m.

A.tricolor cultivars may also bear darker hues amongst the three colours.

AMORPHOPHALLUS

Devil's tongue is a genus of over 90 species. Found in moist shaded habitats in tropical Africa and Asia. It is a most interesting plant, but perhaps one you would not wish to grow in your garden even if you could provide the ideal conditions for it. The large, magnificent spathes are unpleasantly scented to attract pollinators, which is a pity because it is a striking plant. They are frost tender and if you wish to grow malodorous plants in your greenhouse, here is one to try. They can be placed outdoors once danger of frost is passed.

CULTIVATION
Dormant tubers should be planted in late winter or early spring at a depth of 10cm (4"). The other deterrent to growing this enormous plant under glass is that you will need plenty of room, a very large container will be required to accommodate the corm-like rhizomes which can be 50cm (20") across. Position in filtered light. Water freely when in growth, applying a balanced liquid fertiliser once a month. Reduce watering as the foliage dies down. Tubers can be overwintered in warm, barely moist conditions.
A humus-rich soil is required outdoors in partial shade.

PROPAGATION
Sow seed in autumn or early spring. Separate offsets when dormant.

A.konjac has reddish-purple spathes with a dark brown spadix. 13°C (55°F).

A.titanum has reddish-purple spathes to 1.5m (5ft) long, each with a white protruding spadix on 1m (3ft) long stalks.

ANEMONE

Of over 120 perennials in this genus from a wide range of habitats in temperate regions, the species described below offer bronzed foliage. These are fully hardy.

CULTIVATION
Varies according to the species.

PROPAGATION
Seed is best sown as soon as ripe, germination may be slow or erratic. Clump-forming species can be divided and tubers separated.

A. x lipsiensis offers finely cut bronzed leaves with sulphur yellow flowers held well above the foliage in April. A woodland species. 15cm. Grow in moist but well-drained, humus-rich soil in partial shade. Will tolerate drier conditions when dormant in summer.

A.ranunculoides 'Superba' is a spreading perennial with deeply lobed, deeply divided bronzed leaves. Solitary deep yellow flowers open in spring. Cultivation as the above species.

ANGELICA

Excellent ornamental with architectural value in the garden. Suitable for positioning by a stream or in damp woodland. Fully hardy.

CULTIVATION
Grow in deep, moist, fertile loamy soil in full or partial shade.

PROPAGATION
Sow fresh seed in a cold frame, needs exposure to light to germinate. Transplant seedlings when small, they will flower in 2-3 years.

A.atropurpurea is an interesting foliage plant, suitable for the border. New growth appears with red stems and rich claret and green foliage. Leaves mature to mid-green with red veining. Clusters of white umbellifer flowers appear in summer. 1.2 to 2m (4-6ft).

A.gigas is a biennial producing domed umbellifer flower heads of an astonishing deep beetroot from mid to late summer on thick branching stems. Save the seed. Not for limy soils. 1.2m (4ft).

A.sylvestris 'Purpurea' is an impressive plant which has leaves, stems and flowers suffused purple, seeds freely so select the best blackish-brownish foliage. Flowers from June through to September. 2m (6ft).

A.'Vicar's Mead' is similar to the above but not as architectural nor as dark. It bears dark foliage with pink flowers but can be variable.

ANTHRISCUS

Like a dark Cow parsley, makes an attractive foliage plant. Good contrast in the herbaceous border. Fully hardy.

CULTIVATION
Any well-drained soil will suit in sun or partial shade.

PROPAGATION
Sow seed in spring or autumn. Select the best dark foliage.

A.sylvestris 'Ravenswing', has wonderful dark chocolate foliage which provides good colour contrast for the border. The small white flowers are produced in late spring to summer. Self-seeding may become a nuisance if not dead-headed. 1m (3ft).

ANTHURIUM

The Flamingo flower is a large genus of over 700 species of evergreen perennials many of which are epiphytic. They are found in the tropics and subtropics normally in wet mountain forests. Leaves are often glossy and you could be forgiven for thinking the whole plant is made of plastic. Brightly coloured spathes and cylindrical spadices are a feature. In frost prone areas they can be grown in containers indoors. Cut flowers are exceptionally long-lasting. They are frost tender.

CULTIVATION
The crowns should be planted just above the soil surface and covered with a layer of sphagnum moss. Roots must not be allowed to dry out.
Indoors, grow in epiphytic compost. High humidity and temperature are essential. Water freely in the growing season in filtered light, moving to full light in winter when watering needs to be greatly reduced. Apply a balanced feed every 2-3 weeks when in growth. Top dress annually and pot on every 2 years. 16°C (61°F).

PROPAGATION
Seed may take several months to germinate. Plants may be divided in winter. Stem cuttings or offsets can be rooted in spring or summer.

A.crystallinum has very dark green leaves, with light green veins. Stunning.

A.'Violet Tapers' has a bright violet spadix with a small pearl spathe stained violet.
A. 'Negrito' has dark green leaves, arrow-shaped at the base to 30cm (1ft) long. Erect, rounded-ovate, deep copper spathes 7-12cm (3-5") long with purple spadices are borne throughout the year. 60 cm (24").
A.wilfordii , the chocolate bird's nest bears new leaves of claret, maturing into succulent mahogany cocoa tones. Sounds like one for chocolate lovers.

ANTIRRHINUM

The Snapdragons make up a genus of about 30-40 species. They include annuals, perennials and sub-shrubs from mainly rocky sites in Europe, USA and N.Africa. Grown for their lovely tubular, lipped flowers which are produced from early summer to autumn. Branching stems bear linear or ovate leaves.
The common Snapdragon, A.majus is usually grown as a bedding annual even though it is a short-lived perennial. This species is fully hardy.

CULTIVATION
Grow A.majus in fertile soil in full sun. Soil needs to be sharply drained. Prolong flowering by dead-heading.

PROPAGATION
Sow seed of A.majus cultivars in autumn or spring. The tiny seed needs to be sown thinly, seedlings often damp off. Select the best dark foliage forms.

A. majus 'Black Prince' has long been a favourite of mine, with that all too rare combination of good dark foliage and appealing dark flowers. In a good form the foliage approaches black and the flowers are a very dark, deep red. Eye-catching when planted en masse. If you only grow one Antirrhinum, make it this one. I would advise you to sow each year or take cuttings from the darkest forms. Antirrhinums can be prone to rust.

AQUILEGIA

Around 70 perennials make up this genus, but only a few species offer dark flowers or foliage. Found in meadow, woodland and mountainous areas of the northern hemisphere. They produce basal rosettes of mainly lobed leaves. Flowers are distinctive, bell-shaped on the whole. The many forms of A.vulgaris are suitable in light woodland and are effective in the herbaceous border. They cross-pollinate readily. They are fully hardy.

CULTIVATION
Grow in fertile, moist but well-drained soil in full sun or partial shade. Alpine species will need a gritty, well-drained soil.

PROPAGATION
Preferably obtain seed as soon as ripe and sow immediately in the cold frame, otherwise sow in spring. A period of cold stratification may help.
Cultivars can be divided, but do resent disturbance.

A.grata is a beautiful species from Yugoslavia with deep mauve blue inky-violet flowers in spring. 30-45cm (12-18").

A.karelinii is a wonderful plant bearing numerous very dark violet flowers that make an immediate impression. 60cm (2ft). **A.secundiflora** is quite rare and also bears small violet flowers with spurs above delicate lacy foliage. 30cm (12").

A.'Roman Bronze' is a dark flowered counterpart to Aquilegia 'Mellow-Yellow'. The foliage opens yellow, but soon darkens to an orange-bronze. Flowers are quite consistently deep violet. An exceptional recent introduction. Discard any seedlings with paler foliage. 60cm (2ft).

A.vulgaris v stellata 'Black Barlow' is a black version of the better-known and curiously fascinating A.vulgaris v stellata 'Nora Barlow' with purple-black blooms.This is a double-flowered variety. 90cm (3ft).

Perhaps one of the most well-known black plants is **A.vulgaris 'William Guiness'** which many nurseries and seed suppliers sell under the synonym of Magpie. Dense clouds of puckered deepest blue-black and white flowers abound on this attractive Granny's Bonnet. For impact plant in small groups of 3-5 plants. 60-90cm (2-3ft).

There are now doubles on the market too, if you prefer the fussier look to the simplicity of the single flower. Frilly, double black and white. **A.vulgaris 'William Guiness Doubles**' stand at 60-90cm (2-3ft).

There is also **A.vulgaris v flore-pleno black**, an intriguing dark double-flowered variety.

A.viridiflora is a choice and unusual plant from Siberia which produces delicate sprays of very sweetly perfumed green skirted flowers with intriguing maroon-brown or chocolate purple centres which form a perfect contrast with the yellow anthers. One seed firm market this as 'Chocolate Soldier', but it is none other than A.viridiflora. 30cm (12").

ARISAEMA

These members of the aroid family form a genus of about 150 species of tuberous or rhizamatous perennials from moist woodland and rocky wasteland. The unusual, interesting spathes are what attracts the black plant enthusiast. The spathes are stunning and quite a number of them are in deep purple, brownish shades. They also have attractive lobed or palmate green leaves. They are fully to half hardy and when grown outside are best in partial shade. Give protection in frost-prone areas for tender species.

CULTIVATION

Tubers or rhizomes should be planted at a depth of 15-25cm (6-10") in winter or spring in humus-rich soil. Under glass, grow in deep pots in leaf mould, grit and loam in bright, indirect light. Mulch in winter and protect from late spring frosts. Never allow dormant tubers to dry out completely.

PROPAGATION

Sow seed in containers in autumn or spring in a cold frame. If species produce offsets, these can be removed and potted up in late summer.

These are some of my favourite plants and if I were lucky enough to be granted four wishes, you can see my choice below.

A.amurense is a tuberous perennial, usually bearing a solitary leaf divided into lance-shaped leaflets. On a purple stem it produces hooded spathes 8-12cm (3-5") long, each strikingly marked with dark purple and white stripes in spring. 45cm (18").

A.ciliatum bears clean brown and white striped Arum flowers from June to July. Enormous, decorative parasol leaves appear later and get bigger every year.

A.costatum is a tuberous perennial which has deep purple-brown spathes with white stripes, 10-15cm (4-6") long. The single, red-margined leaf is divided. 40cm(16").

A.elephas has a green leaf divided into leaflets. The spathe is around 15cm (6") long and deep purple with white stripes at the base. The spadix develops a long, curved purple appendage which extends to the ground. A delightful Chinese species.

A.griffithii, if allowed four wishes, this would be it. One of the most unusual of the Arisaemas, it has to be seen to be believed. In April-May large dark purple spathes appear, veined delicately with white and hooded. This tuberous perennial also produces two large leaves, divided and themselves veined. Exceptionally striking. Up to 60cm (2ft).

A.kishidae is a hardy species of the serratum group, with two divided leaves and a rusty-reddish-brown flower, with a long-extended spathe tip and a club-like spadix. There is a rare selection of the above with a splash of silver in the centre of each leaf. An absolute gem and little charmer.

A.kiushianum bears a single leaf to 30cm (12") tall with 7-13 leaflets. The spathe is dark purple with white markings on the inside. The spadix is like a mouse tail up to 15cm (6") long.

A.lobatum is only recently introduced into Great Britain. The spathes are a lightish brown, with white, and the shiny green leaves appear after flowering. Not the darkest, but nevertheless superb. 30cm (12").

A.maximowiczii has a dark purple stem, the spathe being green sometimes purple, striped white. Rare.

A.purpureogalatum occasionally appears in nursery or seed listings, it displays a deep purple-black hood with a slender tail almost 30cm (12") long.

A.ringens, the true species (it is also a synonym for A. robustum which has green spathes) bears a large hooded and curled green and purple-striped, purple-lipped spathe 10-15cm long. 30cm (12").

A.sazensoo is sometimes wrongly listed as a synonym of A.sikokianum, it does not have a bulbous spadix, and the purple spathe hood drops way down over the tube.

If the one photograph I have seen of **A.serratum** is to be believed, this is my number one choice from this genus. A sumptuous, very desirable, black silky spathe that conjures up images of sexy black satin underwear and sex at midnight. It has real wow impact. Opulently rich, very dark, near-black spathes can be produced on this northeast Asian species. A startling white, golf-ball like spadix is displayed against the truly magnificent spathe. Try to see it in flower, because unfortunately, it can be variable and produce green spathes, or spathes only spotted or striped purple. If only someone out there could select the darkest black-purple form and, if possible try to produce it consistently, we should all be in heaven. Ultimately desirable and breathtakingly beautiful. Tender, needs protection. 1m (3ft).

If I were allowed three wishes, after the species below, my choice would be **A.sikokianum**. The deep purple spathe surrounds a striking club-shaped pure white spadix to give perfect contrast. Commands attention. This tuberous perennial is borderline hardy. 30-50cm (12-20").

Second on my list would be the most attractive **A.speciosum**. Its long, slender spathes are purple with white stripes deep into the throat. A single 3-palmate leaf is borne at the same time of flowering in late spring to summer. This species needs protection from frost. 60cm (24").

A.ternatipartitum is a diminutive and very rare species with 3-parted leaves, and 'ears' on the brown spathe. Good for a trough and forms colonies.

A.triphyllum, commonly known as Jack-in-the-pulpit produces stately spathes of green on the outside with purplish-brown inside. This species flowers in summer. 15-60cm (6-24"). Again, it can, unfortunately be variable and will sometimes produce only green spathes. A hardy species and the one with perhaps the most attractive leaves.

ARISARUM

Most species of this genus of rhizomatous or tuberous perennials bear purplish spathes. Found in moist woodland or rocky ground and wasteland in Europe. They are grown for their hooded spathes which appear in winter to mid-spring. Fully to half hardy.

CULTIVATION
Tubers or rhizomes should be planted at a depth of 8cm (3") in autumn in humus-rich soil. Indoors, pot up into gritty, humus-rich, loamless potting compost and place in filtered light.

PROPAGATION
Sow seed in a cold frame in spring. Divide in autumn or winter.

A.kiusianum is a clump-forming evergreen species with leaves to 7.5cm (3") long, usually patterned. Bears 3-lobed flowers of brownish purple.

A.kiusianum v tubulosum bears cafe au lait to white flowers, perhaps one for milk chocolate lovers.

A.maximum, the Panda Asarum, bears black flowers to 5cm (2") across with a pure white eye. Lush, evergreen leaves to 18cm (7") long are glossy and faintly patterned. Suitable for a cold greenhouse or outdoors in warmer climates. (Asiatica).

A.megacalyx has wide-ranging rhizomes, glossy evergreen leaves to 7.5cm (3") long being dark green or patterned. Bears large, bell-shaped nearly black flowers. Does well in loose, humus-rich soil.

A.nipponicum is now rare in the wild. It has leathery oval leaves of green, or grey-green, which are usually patterned to 10cm (4") long. It bears small brown flowers in winter. Excellent in shade.

A.proboscideum is the easiest species to obtain. Mats of attractive arrow-shaped, glossy green leaves, approximately 10cm (4") long almost hide the blackish maroon or brownish purple spathes with long, thin curled tips like whips which are commonly referred to as mousetails. They do indeed give the appearance of mice scurrying away to hide. A rhizomatous perennial, it requires a humus-rich soil in partial shade and is fully hardy. Flowers are produced from February to March. It is capable of forming large colonies of low carpets which provide attractive edging for a woodland setting. 15cm (6").

A.simile is extremely rare with oval-triangular leaves which are dark green and velvety, usually unmarked. It bears brownish flowers with undulate lobes.

A.thunbergii comes from the southern islands of Japan and has much-divided glossy leaves and a very long black whip-like spadix snaking out from the purple-brown spathe. Dramatic.

A.vulgare is a tuberous perennial with arrow-shaped leaves of mid to yellowish green, smaller than the above, but are sometimes attractively mottled purple. In winter or spring, small green hooded spathes are produced which are striped brown or purple, with blackish-brown spadices. It is a tender subject more suited to the alpine house. 10cm (4").

ARISTOLOCHIA

If you are looking for unusual flowers, this genus provides them in shades of purple. Over 300 species of mainly evergreen and deciduous climbers are included in this genus. Found mainly in moist woodland in temperate and tropical regions of both hemispheres. Attractive, often heart-shaped leaves and petalless flowers in shades of white, purple, liver-brown or maroon, veined or mottled with dark hues are the features of this remarkable and extraordinary genus. Too good to be true? The down side is that some have unpleasant smelling flowers, so choose with care. They are fully hardy to frost tender.

CULTIVATION

A loamless compost will suit them under glass in bright filtered light. Water freely when in growth and apply a balanced feed every month. Little water is needed in winter. Outdoors grow in fertile soil in sun or partial shade. Hardy species overwinter best in dry soils. Give climbers strong support and prune after flowering in spring, pruning back to 2 or 3 nodes.

PROPAGATION

Sow seed as soon as ripe or in spring. Divide perennials in spring or take root cuttings in winter. Root softwood cuttings of climbing or scandent species grown under glass in early spring, and of hardy species in midsummer.

A.californica is a deciduous, vigorous climber which can reach 4.5m(15ft) or more. It bears heart-shaped leaves and small, dull purple flowers with the upper lip divided into 2 lobes. Will require protection in frost prone areas.

A.gigantea is a tender evergreen twiner with dark green heart-shaped leaves. The flowers are solitary purple with white veins or maroon and are borne in summer. They are large to 15cm (6") across. Minimum temperature 10°C (50°F). 10m (30ft).

Another species bearing large flowers, as its name suggests, is **A.grandiflora.** Unfortunately, the purple and green flowers emit a strong odour to attract pollinating flies which is anything but appealing. Tender. 10m (30ft) or more.

A.littoralis is a fast-growing creeper native to Brazil, as such it will need high humidity and frost protection. It produces highly attractive purple flowers which are veined white, similar in colouring to A.gigantea. The veined markings are stronger and there is a purple band deep in the throat of the flower which is of a different shape to the latter species. These are borne in summer and are an interesting shape which is often likened to a pipe, hence the common name of the genus of Dutchman's pipe, although this species is more commonly referred to as the Calico flower. It can be grown as an annual in cool climates and requires a minimum temperature of 7°C (54°F). 5-8m (15-25ft).

A.macrophylla is a strong grower and will crowd out other species as it grows, so be careful where you position this plant. It has dark green heart-shaped leaves which tend to cover the pipe-shaped flowers which are green, mottled purple or brown 8-10m (25-30ft). Borderline hardy.

ARTEMISIA

Over 300 species of mixed classification make up this genus of plants. Found in northern temperate regions as well as S.America and Southern Africa. Just one has dark foliage. It is fully hardy.

CULTIVATION
Easy, preferably in moist soil.

PROPAGATION
Sow seed in a cold frame in autumn or spring.

A.lactiflora Guizhou Group has dense sprays of white flowers contrasting beautifully with the mahogany stems above blackish finely cut fragrant foliage. More or less true from seed. Eye-catching, especially in full sun. 90cm (3ft).

ARTHROPODIUM

A dozen perennials from Australasia make up this genus. Mostly with broad grassy foliage and racemes of flowers. Frost hardy to -10°C (14°F) in a sheltered spot with good drainage.

CULTIVATION
Fertile, well-drained gritty soil in full sun in a sheltered position. Under glass, use loam-based compost with added sand.

PROPAGATION
Sow seed in a cold frame, autumn or early spring. Divide in spring.

A.candidum 'Maculatum' and **'Purpureum'** are usually seed-raised forms which bear bronze foliage. Overwinter young plants under glass.

ARUM

Curious and interesting are the words to describe this genus. These tuberous perennials are found in partially shaded habitats in S.Europe. Attractively shaped and marked leaves are a feature of many species. They are fully to half hardy.

CULTIVATION
Tubers should be planted at a depth of 10-15cm (4-6") in autumn or spring. Choose a position in partial shade or full sun in well-drained, humus-rich soil. Under glass grow in loamless compost with added grit, in full or filtered light. In growth, water freely and apply a balanced feed monthly. Reduce watering as the leaves wither and keep almost dry when dormant.

PROPAGATION
Sow seed in autumn in a cold frame, first removing the pulp from the berries, wearing gloves. Divide after flowering.

Both **A.dioscoridis and A.hygrophilum** have spathes marked or flushed dark purple, the spathes of the former being green or maroon purple and of the latter green.
A.dioscoridis v smithii has deep maroon splashes and dots on flat, open creamy spathes in April to May.
There is also a black spotted form of A.italicum.
A.maculatum 'Pleddel' has dark maroon spotted leaves and the pale green spathes are marked with the same hue.
A.nigrum has a dark purple-brown spathe and spadix.
A.palaestinum steals the limelight here with its near-black spathes and spadix. The outer spathe is greenish white. It does have a musty smell. 45cm (18"). It flowers at the end of spring and is a tender subject.

ASARUM

Leaves are large, often marbled and conceal pitcher-shaped flowers which have a faintly unpleasant odour, being mostly brownish-purple. Good for ground cover and edging, suitable for shade or woodland. Fully hardy, may be found to shed their leaves at temperatures below -15°C (5°F).

CULTIVATION
Grow in partial to full shade in moderately fertile, humus-rich soil, moist but well-drained. They prefer neutral to acid soil.

PROPAGATION
Sow fresh seed in a cold frame. Divide in early spring.

A.arifolium is a variable species with large, elongated, heart-shaped leaves up to 15cm (6") long, marked with lighter green. The purple flowers are borne at ground level.

A.asaroides has large, tubby brown flowers. Easy in shade. Grey-green leaves have cloudy silver patterns which take on a rose blush in winter.

A.canadense, wild ginger is an evergreen prostrate perennial with a slender, aromatic rhizome which smells of ginger. It has green, hairy, heart-shaped leaves and urn-shaped purple-brown flowers near ground level in spring. 8cm (3").

A.caudatum is native to the coastal mountains of western America. It is a ground-hugging evergreen perennial which grows in deep shade on the forest floor. Spreading by rhizomes in patches, it flowers from late spring into summer. Large, kidney-shaped leaves rise to 20cm (8") above the ground, hiding the purplish-brown flowers below.

A.celsum is a very rare, clump-forming evergreen species with variable leaves, usually unmarked, and purple-brown flowers with rings and ridges.

A.dimidiatum is a rarely seen deciduous Japanese species with bright green leaves and dark purple, nearly black flowers.

A.dissitum has handsome foliage, almost glossy or velvety often with white spots and bears small, brownish tubular flowers.

A.europaeum, Asarabacca, has small, narrowly bell-shaped greenish purple then brown flowers.

A.hartwegii has the added advantage of dark green-bronze leaves with broadly tubular brownish-purple flowers.

A.hatsusimae has white-tipped brownish flowers perched on stems unusually held above the ground.

A.magnificum has superb large flowers of white and brownish-black in spring.

A.maximum has black throated, white centred, black tri-lobed flowers to 6cm wide.

A.shuttleworthii and **A.splendens** also bear purple-brown flowers.

ASTER

A.lateriflorus has foliage which turns copper in autumn.

A.lateriflorus 'Lady in Black' has stunning near black foliage which makes a feature throughout summer before the small beige/purple flowers appear in late autumn. A more open form than the one below. 120cm (4ft).

A.lateriflorus 'Prince' has deep bronze to black purple foliage and stems with pale pink flowers in autumn. It offers good contrast with pink flowered plants. It can be used effectively as a hedge. 60cm. (2ft).

CULTIVATION
Well-drained, open, moderately fertile soil in full sun.

PROPAGATION
Sow seed in a cold frame in spring or autumn or divide in spring or autumn.

ASTILBE

Around 12 species of rhizomatous perennials mainly from moist sites in eastern Asia. They form basal tufts of ferny, compound leaves, with sharply toothed leaflets. They have striking, plume-like panicles of flowers. Excellent for woodland or by a stream. They are fully hardy.

CULTIVATION
Light shade will suit them best, with a rich, leafy soil that never dries out. In boggy sites they can even be grown in full sun. Divide every 3 years.

PROPAGATION
Divide in winter or early spring when dormant. Species seed is available.

A.x arendsii 'Cattleya' bears young bronze foliage with rose-pink flowers.
A.x arendsii 'Ellie van Veen' bears purple-bronze foliage and white flowers.
A. x arendsii 'Obergartner Jurgens' is a new variety with remarkably dark foliage which contrasts well with the red flowers. 60cm (2ft).
A. 'Bronce Elegans' (simplicifolia hybrid) is a beautiful dwarf form with green foliage darkened with bronze shadows which makes a good base for the arching sprays of tiny flowers in cream and salmon pink. Flowers appear in July and August. 30cm (1ft).
A.glaberrima also has bronzed leaves.
A.glaberrima v saxatilis is more widely grown, producing deep green leaves, red-tinted on the undersides. Spikes of white-tipped mauve flowers are borne in summer. Thrives in moist soil. 8cm (3").
A. x crispa 'Perkeo' has dark green mature leaves on bronze stems with rose-pink flowers. Foliage is also bronze-tinted when young. A small hybrid. 20cm (8").

ATRIPLEX

About 100 species of annuals, perennials and shrubs make up this genus. It can be found world-wide in both temperate and warm regions. A. hortenis is salt-tolerant. There are quite a few cultivars which offer different colourings from the green of the species.

CULTIVATION
Species can thrive in poor to moderate soil, with the exception of A.hortensis which enjoys fertile, moist soil, well-drained in full sun. Water well in dry periods to reduce the tendency to bolt.

PROPAGATION
Sow seed in situ in succession from spring to early summer.

A. hortensis v rubra is a useful and easily grown foliage plant which comes true from seed. It is decorative as well as edible and rapid growing and can be used in the border, or in summer bedding schemes. Orach has beetroot red or purple-red leaves, stems and flower spikes. 60cm - 1.2m (2-4ft).

ATROPA

Deep purple flowers are to be found on this notorious plant.

A plant that needs little introduction is **A.belladonna,** Deadly nightshade has purple-brown, bell-shaped flowers. After flowering in summer, shiny, black berries are produced. Mainly grown these days as a curiosity or for educational use. Propagate from seed. 1-1.5m (3-5ft).

All parts are poisonous and narcotic.

BEGONIA

A large genus of over 900 species of which the rex hybrids and semperflorens begonias offer deeply bronzed or purple foliage nearing black.

Begonia rex are mainly rhizomatous perennials cultivated for their foliage, bright light enhances the darker colours, whilst lower light brings out the metallic sheen often found on the attractive, evergreen leaves. Maintain a temperature of 21-24°C (70-75°F). Direct sunlight will scorch leaves and do try to avoid splashing leaves when watering.

Begonia semperflorens is a species of fibrous-rooted evergreen perennials. Bushy and fairly compact, they are normally used as annuals in summer bedding schemes, overwinter them indoors or under glass in cold areas. Some species have green leaves, others have been developed with deep bronze leaves which contrast beautifully with the flowers in shades of white, pink, salmon and red. They are good for partial shade. Overwinter at a minimum of 10°C (50°F).

CULTIVATION

Keep just moist and allow B.rex to dry out a little between watering, rhizome rot can be a problem if they are too wet.

PROPAGATION

Both species can be grown from seed. Seed is very fine and high temperatures are needed for germination. B.rex can also be propagated by rhizome sections and by leaf cuttings. B.semperflorens can be propagated by basal cuttings.

BEGONIA REX -TYPES

B.'Beatrice Haddrell' has star-shaped almost black leaves with green veins. Pink flowers are freely produced in winter.

B.'Bokit' has black and red spiral leaves.

B.'Ebony' has dark green leaves with mahogany undersides.

B.'Filigree' is pink on satin black.

B.'Helen Lewis' has silver-banded dark wine-red leaves.

B.'Helen Teupel' has long, jagged dark purple-black leaves with splashes of silver and pink.

B.'Razzamatazz' is a medium-sized plant with spiral leaves, satiny red with black centre and margins.

B.'Red Robin' is compact with smallish, heart-shaped red leaves with a contrasting matt black centre and edge. Striking.

B.'Tiny Bright' has red, green and bronze bands.

B.'Vesuvius' is a medium-sized plant with black foliage with red interveinal marking. Quite remarkable.

BEGONIA SEMPERFLORENS

The **Doublet Series** has bronze-purple foliage, with stunning double-white flowers which give a perfect contrast. Also available in pink and red flowered forms. There are many from seed including The **Victory Series, 'Coco'** and F1 **'Cocktail'** , F1 **'Expresso'** and F1 **'Partydress'** all offer a mix of flower colour with bronze foliage. The **F1 'Whisky'** also offers bronze foliage with the striking contrast of white flowers, as does F1 **'Ambra'**. There are also mixes of green and bronze foliage.

TUBEROUS BEGONIAS

A recent introduction from seed is **'Midnight Beauty Orange'**. Dark chocolate, almost black foliage is crowned with masses of fully double, rich orange blooms. 25cm (10").

BERBERIS

The 450 species of this genus of evergreen or deciduous shrubs are found throughout the northern hemisphere. They offer some good purple foliage which can be used as a backdrop for smaller plants. They can also make an effective hedge. Some are frost hardy, however all those below are fully hardy.

CULTIVATION
Any well-drained soil in full sun for fruiting and autumn colour.

PROPAGATION
Sow seed in a seedbed in early spring. Garden seed will probably result in hybrids as they cross easily. Take semi-ripe cuttings in summer.

B.thunbergii f atropurpurea is perhaps the best known of the purple-leaved barberries. It produces dark-red purple or purplish bronze foliage turning a metallic bronze-black in the autumn. 1m (3ft) or more.
B.thunbergii 'Atropurpurea Nana' is a dwarfer, neat, rounded shaped form of the above, with some greenish tints in the foliage. 45cm (18").
B. thunbergii 'Bagatelle' is a very compact form with shiny deep purple foliage which turns red in autumn. 30cm (12").
B.thunbergii 'Dart's Red Lady' has very dark purplish red foliage which turns brighter red in autumn. 80cm (32").
B.thunbergii 'Golden Ring' is a little different from the others in that its light purple foliage is very narrowly margined with golden yellow, turning rich red in autumn.
B.thunbergii 'Helmond Pillar' is a narrowly upright form and therefore a good choice for restricted space. It has dark

red-purple foliage. 1m (3ft).
B.thunbergii 'Red Chief' is a taller form which has shiny dark purple leaves, with contrasting yellow flowers in spring. 1.5m (4.5ft).
B.thunbergii 'Red Pillar' is an upright, deciduous shrub with reddish-purple foliage which turns crimson in autumn. An improvement on the earlier cultivar 'Erecta'. 1-1.3m (3-4ft).
B.thunbergii 'Rose Glow' is a variegated variety but the variegation does not show until the second season. The leaves are a good rich purple with pinkish/whitish variegation. Best hard-pruned each March. 1.5m (4.5ft).

Berberis x ottawensis f purpurea is a vigorous form with red-purple foliage.
B. x ottawensis 'Silver Miles' is an attractive purple-leaved Barberry with silver variegation, turning red in autumn.
B. x ottawensis 'Superba' is a clonal selection from B. x ottawensis f purpurea which has purple-red foliage which turns crimson in autumn. A deciduous shrub with densely massed stems useful for hedging and prized by flower arrangers. It is similar to, but taller than B.thunbergii f atropurpurea and more vigorous. New growth is bronze red and it bears yellow flowers. 1.8m (6ft).

B.vulgaris 'Atropurpurea' is a purple-leaved form of the common hedgerow species.

BERGENIA

There are 6-8 species in this genus to be found in Central or E.Asia. These semi-evergreen perennials of the saxifrage family are characterised by their large, elephant ear leaves, which rise from the ground on short stalks. Many hybrids offer purplish foliage, especially in winter. Flowers are mainly pink, some white and are an added attraction too. Ideal for woodland gardens and borders. They are fully to frost hardy.

CULTIVATION

A position in humus-rich, moist but well-drained soil in full sun or partial shade is most suitable. Winter leaf colour is enhanced by exposure and poor soil. They will benefit from a mulch in autumn.

PROPAGATION

Garden seed will give rise to hybrids. Divide clumps every 4 years in autumn or spring.

B.'Abendglut' is a clump-forming perennial with rosettes of roundish foliage with crinkled edges. Red-tinted dark green leaves, ruby red beneath. 15cm (6") long. These turn a rich maroon in winter. Magenta-crimson semi-double flowers in spring. 20-30cm (8-12").

B.'Admiral' is one of the best for winter colour with bronze and crimson tints. Cherry pink flowers are held well above the foliage in spring. 30cm.

B.'Ballawley' has broadly ovate glossy green leaves which redden and are turned bronze-purple by frost. Prefers a sheltered position. The name is only to be used for plants which are vegetatively reproduced, seed-raised plants should be known as Ballawley Hybrids. 61cm (24").

B.'Bressingham Ruby' makes neat clusters of spoon-shaped leaves with serrated edges. Winter colour is superb being a polished dark burgundy which contrasts with the lighter crimson undersides. Deep rose flowers in spring. 60cm (24").

B.'Bressingham Salmon' has obovate, bronze-tinted green leaves which turn dark-red in winter.

B.cordifolia 'Purpurea' has redder leaves than the species with rhubarb red stalks. The odd one may turn bright red in summer, and by autumn they are burnished with purplish-red. 46cm (20").

B.crassifolia also has large attractive purple foliage in winter. It is a very tolerant species withstanding severe weather.

B.'Eric Smith' is valued for its winter effect when its large, crinkled leaves have polished bronze-tinted surfaces. In low sunlight, the reverse of the leaves glow a rich carmine-red. 46cm (18").

B.'Eroica' slender red-stained stems rise above the foliage which colours well in autumn with maroon undersides and bright cherry surfaces. 60-75cm (24-30").

B.'Mrs.Crawford' also offers good winter tones of rich plum and crimson against contrasting white flowers. 25-30cm (10-12").

Or you could plant up B. purpurascens which gives good winter colour of deep purple or beetroot red especially in frost, enhanced by reddish-brown stems. There is a Helen Dillon form which offers light-reddish bronze colour in winter.

B.'Pugsley's Pink' has large glossy leaves which are suffused with dark bronze-red tones in winter, accentuated by crimson stems. 60cm (24").

BETULA

Of the 60 species of Birch there is not much to attract the attention of the dark plant lover. Most do have wonderful ornamental bark and some are very suitable for the smaller garden. These fully hardy trees are tolerant of exposed sites.

CULTIVATION
Moderately fertile, moist but well-drained soil in full sun or light dappled shade.

PROPAGATION
Can be raised from seed, but may produce hybrids as they cross easily. It is far better to obtain seed of specified wild origin. Sow in a seedbed in autumn. Root softwood cuttings in summer. Graft in winter.

B.lenta has dark red bark which may be of interest.

B.nigra, the Black Birch will not satisfy the yearning for dark plants of black or purple hue. Its luxuriant, triangular leaves are mid to dark green, turning yellow in autumn. The bark is where the name comes from - shaggy red-brown bark which peels in layers when young and is most attractive. On older specimens, the bark becomes blackish or greyish white and fissured. Mature trees fork into several limbs. Its natural habitat is beside rivers, which gives the other common name of River Birch. 18m (60ft).

B.pendula 'Purpurea' fits the bill a little better with its purple-tinged bark and the coveted rich dark-purple leaves. Slow growing. 10m (30ft).

BIARUM

An unusual genus of 15 species of tuberous perennials mainly from the Mediterranean and W.Asia. In autumn they produce spathes which can be malodorous. The species described need to be grown in a bulb frame, with the exception of B.tenuifolium. Both seed and plants can be difficult to obtain.

CULTIVATION
Dormant tubers need to be planted at a depth of 5cm (2"). They will do well in equal parts of loam, leaf mould and grit in full light. Keep warm and dry when dormant, water sparingly in growth.

PROPAGATION
Sow seed at 13°C (55°F) in autumn or spring. Prick out seedlings as soon as possible. Divide tubers in summer.

B.dispar bears dark purple-brown spathes with a purple spadix.

B.eximium is a tuberous perennial bearing large, dark purple spathes and near-black spadices at ground level in autumn. Spathes are followed by the leaves. 8-10cm (3-4").

B.ochridense bears small purple brown and green spathes from September to October. 8cm (3").

B.tenuifolium is perhaps somewhat easier to grow as it is hardy and can be grown outside at the base of a sunny wall. It has narrow, often twisted pale green spathes which are flushed purple and bears nearly black spadices in autumn. 10-20cm (4-8").

BORONIA

Boronia megastigma has interesting brownish purple flowers on the outside with yellowish inners. It is a tender, dense shrub with aromatic leaves which may survive short periods of frost. 1-3m (3-10ft).

CULTIVATION
Under glass, grow in lime free compost in full light, providing shade from hot sun and adequate ventilation. Water moderately in growth and apply a phosphate-free liquidiser once a month. Pot on or top dress in spring.
Outdoors, grow in well-drained, sandy, neutral to acid soil.

PROPAGATION
Sow seed at 16°C (61°F) in spring. Root semi-ripe cuttings with bottom heat in summer.

BRACHYGLOTTIS

B.repanda 'Purpurea' is a striking small tree of rapid growth in its native country, New Zealand.
The deep glossy purple leaves are wavy at the edges. When cut back, leaves retain a larger size than when allowed to grow into a tree. In late winter to early spring it produces frothy panicles of thousands of small flowers. It is half hardy. 3m (10ft) or more, double in its native land.

CULTIVATION
Best grown in well-drained soil in full sun. It may form an effective hedge or windbreak in coastal areas.

PROPAGATION
Propagate by rooting semi-ripe cuttings in summer.

BUDDLEJA

B.'Black Knight' is the darkest Buddleja on offer.
It bears dense panicles of dark, purple-blue flowers from summer to autumn.
Grow in fertile, well-drained soil in full sun. Excellent plants for attracting butterflies to the garden which has earned them the common name of the butterfly bush. 3m (10ft).

CALYCANTHUS

I find the dusky red flowers of Calycanthus quite captivating.The flowers are unusual and fragrant. Grow in the shrub border or as specimens. Fully hardy.

CULTIVATION
Grow in fertile, moist, humus-rich soil in sun, although they will take partial shade in warm climates. Protect from frost in severe cold winters.

PROPAGATION
Sow fresh seed or sow in autumn in an open frame. Root softwood cuttings in summer, layer in autumn or remove suckers in spring.

C.floridus (Carolina Allspice) bears Magnolia stellata-like flowers with strap-shaped, dark red petals, brownish at the tips in summer. 2.5m (8ft).

C.floridus v glaucus 'Purpureus' will also be of interest with its carmine-red flowers and foliage being tinged purple on the underside.

C.occidentalis (California Allspice) bears similar flowers, both foliage and flowers are larger than C.floridus, the green foliage sometimes yellowing in autumn.3m (10ft).

CAMELLIA

This genus needs little introduction. They provide some darkish reds and are fully hardy to frost tender.

CULTIVATION
Under glass, grow in lime-free potting compost in bright filtered light. In growth, water with soft water. Apply a balanced feed twice during the growing season. Top dress annually. Outdoors, grow in moist, well-drained soil which must be acid and humus-rich. Mulch well. Do not plant deep, the top of the root ball should be level with the firmed soil.

C.'Black Lace' has double, black-red velvet flowers. Rose-form.
C. japonica 'Bob Hope' is a large, upright shrub with dense growth and one of the darkest red flowers of irregular semi-double or peony form. 3m (10ft).
C. japonica 'Dixie Knight' has very dark red semi-double flowers.
C. japonica 'Konronkoku' (Kouron-jura) is also one of the darkest crimson red flowers. My favourite.
C. japonica 'Midnight' has semi-double black-red flowers with yellow stamens. Opinion differs as to which is the darkest, see them in flower if at all possible.

CANNA

Grown for their large, paddle shaped leaves which are often purple and for their equally attractive flowers. In frost prone areas these half hardy plants are useful for summer bedding but the rhizomes will need protection under glass in winter.

CULTIVATION
Grow in loamless potting compost with shade from hot sun under glass. Water freely when in growth and apply a phosphate-rich liquid fertiliser monthly. Outdoors grow in a sheltered site in full sun in fertile soil, watering freely in dry spells. In frost-prone areas lift the rhizomes when frost has blackened the foliage. Store frost-free in barely moist peat or leaf mould. In frost-free areas leave in the ground applying a good winter mulch.

PROPAGATION
Sow chipped or pre-soaked seed in spring or autumn. Divide rhizomes into short sections, in early spring.

C.'Ambassadeur' has purple foliage and clear red flowers.
C.'America' has purple foliage with dark scarlet flowers.
C.'Assaut' has purple-brown leaves and buds, opening into gladiolus-like orange-scarlet flowers. 1.8m (6ft).
C.'Australia' is a superb form.Bears very dark black-red spear shaped leaves with a satin-like sheen and holds its colour well beneath shocking red flowers. 1.2m (4ft).
C.'Black Knight' has bronze foliage with very dark red flowers. 1.8m (6ft).
C.'Durban' (also sold under the names of 'Phaison' and 'Tropicanna') bears purple-maroon leaves with red and yellow stripes and shocking orange flowers. 1-2m (3-6ft).
C.indica 'Purpurea' produces broad, dark purple leaves with bright red or soft orange flowers. 1.5-2.2m (5-7ft).
C.'Intrigue' upright and narrow black-purplish red foliage with apricot-peach flowers. 2.2m (8ft).
C.'King Humbert' has vivid purple leaves and orchid-like bright red flowers. 1.8m.
C.'Louis Cottin' bears dark purple foliage, beware, there is a green one circulating.
C.'Tirol' bears green leaves tinged purple with salmon-pink flowers. 1m (3ft).
C.'Wyoming' has brown-purple foliage with dark purple veins and frilled orange flowers, with apricot feathering. 1.8m (6ft).

CAREX

Sedges are mainly cultivated for their attractive and colourful foliage, some will offer bronzed foliage. Since they are found in very different regions of the world, the differing species can be suited to many sites in the garden. Mostly fully hardy except New Zealand species.

CULTIVATION
Varies according to species.

PROPAGATION
Sow seed of N.Z. species under glass in spring, raise others in a cold frame. Divide between mid-spring and early summer.

C.atrata a native of Europe, including Britain, makes neat tufts of stiff leaves and bears almost black flowerheads on 10cm (4") long stems.
C.berggrenii forms low growing tufts of lovely bronzy brown foliage, in moist but well-drained soil.10cm (4"). Frost hardy.
C.buchananii makes strong, upright clumps of bronze foliage, avoid extremes of wet and dry. 50-75cm (20-30"). Frost hardy.
C.comans bronze form has warm bronze foliage. 25-35cm (10-14cm).
C.dipsacea has black inflorescences with greeny-bronze foliage. 50cm (2ft).
C.flacca has grey-green foliage topped with black flowers in early summer. 20cm.
C.flagellifera is taller and broader than C.comans with purplish-brown foliage. Avoid extremes of wet and dry. 1m (3ft).
C.muskingumensis 'Small Red' is dwarf with tussocks of fine bronze red foliage.
C.plantaginea has wispy black flowers.
C.testacea olive-green foliage, but in full-light the surfaces may appear bronzed. Dark-brown flower spikes. Frost hardy. 1.5m (5ft). Avoid extremes of wet and dry.

CATALPA

Catalpas are usually found on riverbanks. They are known for their handsome foliage and flowers and are often grown as specimen trees. They can offer bronzed foliage when young. They are fully hardy.

CULTIVATION
Fertile, moist but well-drained soil is required as well as shelter from strong winds. Can be pollarded.

PROPAGATION
Sow seed in autumn. Root softwood cuttings in late spring or summer. Graft or insert root cuttings in winter.

C.x erubescens 'Purpurea' has young leaves and shoots of dark purple, almost black which gradually mature to green. White flowers are marked yellow and purple. Spreading habit. 15m (50ft).
C.bignonioides 'Aurea' is bronze when young.

CENTRADENIA

Dark flowers and bronzy foliage combine on this unusual quick-growing plant suitable for indoors cultivation in a pot or hanging basket. Tender species. Minimum temperature 13°C (55°F).

PROPAGATION
Sow seed of species under glass in spring. Root softwood cuttings in spring.

C.inaequilateralis 'Cascade' is a trailing plant with bronze-pink leaves and tibouchina like small violet-purple flowers from May to June and possibly again from August to November. Needs high humidity. 30cm (12").

CENTAUREA

Needing no introduction, **C.nigra** will enhance pink shades with its black buds opening to purple.

A native flower which grows to 60cm (2ft) and worthy of inclusion in a wild area or meadow garden. There was what appeared to be a named cultivar in circulation some time ago 'Black Boy' available form seed, which may be worth seeking. Easy from seed.

C.nigra ssp rivularis has browner buds and is very free-flowering.

CULTIVATION
Best in well-drained soil in full sun.

CERCIDIPHYLLUM

One species of deciduous tree from Japan and China, found in woodland. It offers excellent autumn foliage. Grow as a specimen tree in a woodland setting. Fully hardy, however young leaves may be damaged by frost.

CULTIVATION
Grow in deep, fertile, humus-rich soil, moist but well-drained. It prefers neutral to acid soil and sun or dappled shade in a position sheltered from wind. Can be trained as a standard.

PROPAGATION
The species can be grown from fresh seed, sown in an open frame. Take basal cuttings in late spring and semi-ripe cuttings in midsummer.

C.japonicum 'Rotfuchs' has strong purplish foliage which appears almost black from a distance and offers spectacular autumn colour. 15m (50ft).

CERCIS

One large shrub, or small tree that would surely not disappoint on the colour of its foliage is Cercis canadensis 'Forest Pansy'. Grow young shrubs in the border or trained against a wall. Older trees make good specimens. Fully hardy, but it is a good idea to protect young plants from frost.

CULTIVATION
Grow in fertile, deep, moist but well-drained soil in sun or partial shade. Older plants resent transplanting. Pollarding in spring produces large foliage on already established plants.

PROPAGATION
Sow seed in a cold frame in autumn. Root semi-ripe cuttings in summer.

C.canadensis 'Forest Pansy' has pleasantly attractive heart-shaped leaves of the deepest dark red-purple, in some forms they can appear brownish-bronze. Bears rose-pink flowers from spring to summer. In gardens this will reach to about 3.5m (12ft).

C.canadensis, C.occidentalis and C.siliquastrum (Judas tree) also have bronze-purplish foliage when young.

CHRYSANTHEMUM

The only dark Chrysanthemum I believe you will find is **C.'Black Magic'** an early flowering outdoor reflexed type with dark velvety blooms, darker towards the centre, not perhaps as black as its name suggests, but it does show dark undertones. It is a strong grower with good foliage. Can be disbudded.

CIMICIFUGA

Native to the cooler regions of the northern hemisphere are the 18 species of this genus. These clump-forming perennials are found in moist, shady areas and are suitable for moist borders or woodland. They have compound leaves divided into leaflets and racemes or panicles of bottlebrush-type flowers. They are fully hardy.

CULTIVATION
Grow in moist, humus-rich soil in partial shade.

PROPAGATION
Fresh species seed sown in a cold frame in autumn will germinate the following spring. Divide cultivars in spring.

C.ramosa 'Hillside Black Beauty' is apparently darker than 'Brunette', see below. Described by the American company Wayside Gardens who have sole rights, as the darkest coppery-purple foliage of any Cimicifuga with creamy white bottlebrushes swaying on 1.5m (5ft) stems.Strong fragrance. 60cm (2ft).
C.simplex Atropurpurea Group does well in an open situation in rich, retentive soil, and, unlike other Cimicifugas, its leaves will not scorch. The deeply cut leaves and stems become dark purple, topped in autumn with slender spires of small, sweetly-scented cream flowers. 180cm (6ft).
C.simplex 'Brunette' had the darkest purple foliage and it remains to be seen if it has been superseded by the ramosa hybrid (see above),dark stems and contrasting compact racemes of white flowers.120cm (4ft).
C.simplex 'Elstead' has purple stems and buds which open to white.

CLEMATIS

Needing no introduction, there is one species and a number of interesting hybrids for the dark-plant lover.

CULTIVATION
Grow in fertile, humus-rich, well-drained soil in sun or partial shade. The roots need a cool run. Mulch in late winter.

PROPAGATION
Species can be raised from seed sown as soon as ripe in a cold frame. Layer cultivars in late winter or spring.

C.recta 'Lime Close' has non-vining stems emerging a deep midnight purple in mid-spring gradually fading to green overtones. 120cm (4ft).
C.recta 'Purpurea' has white scented flowers in June-August, and the new foliage is deep purple, turning green as it matures. Will tolerate sun or semi-shade. 2m (6ft).
C.recta 'Velvet Night' has foliage which retains the purple colouring much longer.
C.'Black Madonna' has large deep violet-purple flowers with red stamens in May-June and again in September. 3m (10ft).
C.'Black Prince' is a sinister shade of the deepest purple, fading to reddish purple, in flower from July-September. Almost black on opening. Tolerates sun or shade. This is a chance seedling raised by Alister Keay of New Zealand in 1990 and introduced into the U.K. in 1994. Prune group 3.
C.'Negritjanka' the name means 'African Girl' and is one the darkest purples especially against a light background, with reddish-purple anthers flowering from July to September. Suitable for any aspect. 3m (10ft).
C.'Romantika' has almost black flowers on opening, becoming deepest purple.

CODIAEUM

The variegated leaves of this genus which is commonly known as Croton, come in many enticing hues. Grown in frost-prone areas as houseplants, these plants from Malaysia and the E.Pacific islands can reach 1.5m (5ft). In tropical areas they are grown in shrub borders or as hedges or screens.

CULTIVATION
Grow in a loamless compost in full light but providing shade from hot sun under glass. They require high humidity. Apply a balanced feed every 2 weeks and water freely when in growth, sparingly in winter and using tepid water. Top dress or pot on in spring.
Outdoors grow in fertile, humus-rich, moist but well-drained soil in sun or partial shade. Leggy plants can be cut back.

PROPAGATION
Root softwood cuttings with bottom heat in summer. Air layer in spring.

C.**'Flamingo'** has leaves which are mid-green with cream veins, turning yellow and maturing red or purple.

C.**'Evening Embers'** is dense and strong growing with oval, shallowly lobed leaves of bluish-black 15-25cm (6-10") long, suffused with red and green.

C.**'Mume'** matures to foliage of magenta and purple with emerald green.

C.**'Mortimer'** the piecrust croton has cream-splotched leaves turning crimson-purple as they mature. It has unusual crimped, frilly-edged foliage.

COLOCASIA

Swamp or moist areas of tropical Asia is where you would find the 6 species of these large-leaved deciduous or more or less evergreen perennials. The leaves are attractively arrow-shaped with prominent veins. Flowers can appear at any time (rarely in cultivation) and are delicately fragrant. At least 2 species are grown for their edible fruits. In Hawaii, you could try the glutinous poi or even a taro burger. The former might take some getting used to, but the latter is delicious. They are frost tender plants.

CULTIVATION
Under glass, pot up tubers into loamless potting compost in spring at 18°C (64°F). They require bright, filtered light and high humidity. When in growth, water freely and apply a balanced feed monthly. Keep tubers dry and frost-free when dormant. Outdoors, grow in fertile, humus-rich, moist or even wet, slightly acid soil in partial shade.

PROPAGATION
Divide in winter or early spring.

C.**esculenta 'Black Magic'** is the best form. It is known under many names including C.**'Jet Black Wonder'**, C.**'Cranberry**, C jankensii **'Uahiapele'**. It has huge arrow-shaped leaves about 30cm (1ft) or more long which are a uniformly dark bronze-black on deep purple stems. 2m (6ft). Apparently has been overwintered to 0°F in the U.S. Absolutely stupendous.
C.**'Illustris'** is much smaller and has glorious dark purple leaves with pale veining. 1m (3ft).
C.**'Nigrescens'** has lighter leaves with deep purple veining with an almost leathery

texture to the leaf.

There are other Colocasias of a very deep dark green, blackish green or purplish green, with darker colouring on the undersides of the leaves or green with black staining on the surfaces.Tremendous.

COPROSMA

Coprosmas may be of interest if you are looking for bronzed glossy foliage. The leathery leaves are purple or brown in some of the 90 species that make up this genus mainly from Australasia and S.Pacific. Berries will be produced where plants of both sexes are grown together. Frost hardy to half hardy.

CULTIVATION
Under glass, grow in loam-based potting compost with added grit. They will prefer bright-filtered light with good ventilation. When in growth, water freely and apply a balanced liquid fertiliser monthly. Water moderately at other times of the year. Outdoors, grow in neutral to slightly acid, moderately fertile soil, moist but well-drained. Position in sun or partial shade.

PROPAGATION
Sow seed in a cold-frame in spring. Root semi-ripe cuttings in late summer.

C.brunnera forms good groundcover with chocolate-brown leaves on wiry stems. Translucent blue berries in autumn. 45cm (18"). Frost hardy.
C.'Chocolate Soldier' has very glossy, chocolate-brown to dark green leaves which are marginally larger than the above species. 1m (3ft). Half hardy.
C.'Coppershine' has narrowly, glossy dark-green to purple leaves suffused copper. 1m (3ft). Half hardy.

CORDYLINE
Palm-like shrubs and small trees from S.E.Asia, and the Pacific and Australasia. They make wonderful specimen plants and can be wrapped with hessian or sacking in winter for protection in frost-prone areas. They are half hardy to frost tender.

CULTIVATION
Water moderately in growth under glass in bright, or filtered light. Apply a balanced feed once a month. Water sparingly in winter. Top dress or pot on in spring. Outdoors, grow in fertile, well-drained soil in sun or partial shade.

PROPAGATION
Sow seed in spring. Remove well-rooted suckers in spring.

C.australis 'Atropurpurea' has foliage flushed purple at the base and on the main veins beneath.
C.australis 'Black Tower' is a striking deep reddish-purple.
C.australis 'Pink Stripe' is a deep purple with a central pink bar on each leaf.
C.australis 'Purple Tower' has broad leaves heavily flushed plum-purple.
C.australis 'Purpurea' has slightly paler leaves than the above.
C.australis 'Red Star' and **'Torbay Red'** have reddish purple foliage.
C.fruticosa 'Baby Ti' has foliage suffused copper-red.
C.fruticosa 'Firebrand' is flushed deep red-purple.
C.fruticosa 'Negri' has deep copper-maroon foliage.
C.indivisa 'Purpurea' has leaves suffused bronze-purple.
C.stricta 'Discolor' has bronze-purple leaves .

CORNUS

Dogwoods are found mostly in northern temperate regions. There are 45 species and they offer some interest to the dark plant lover for their autumn colour and winter shoots when grown as pollards.
They are fully to frost hardy.

CULTIVATION
Most species are tolerant of a range of soils and positions. Stems colour best in good light.

PROPAGATION
Sow seed in a seedbed in autumn. Seed sown in spring should be stratified. Root greenwood cuttings in summer. Take hardwood cuttings of those grown for winter shoots in autumn.

C.alba 'Kesselringii' has blackish-purple shoots, leaves turn purplish-red in autumn, **C.controversa ,C.kousa** and cultivars such as **C.k.'Satomi' or the** species **C.mas** and **C.sanguinea** offer purple foliage in autumn.**C.stolonifera 'Kelseyi'** has purplish red twigs.

COROKIA

These evergreen shrubs from New Zealand also offer interesting foliage, they form angular branched patterns which has led to the common name of wire-netting bush. They are reasonably frost hardy, wind tolerant and suit mild coastal climates.

CULTIVATION
Fertile soil, full sun, shelter from winds.

PROPAGATION
Greenwood cuttings early summer.

C.'Coppershine' offers purplish foliage in full sun.
C.x virgata 'Frosted Chocolate' has distinct chocolate coloured foliage in winter.

C.x virgata 'Bronze King' offers bronze-tinted foliage, whilst **C.x virgata 'Bronze Lady'** produces dark bronze leaves. You may also come across **C.cheesemannii 'Chocolate Soldier', 'Winter Bronze'** and others.

CORYDALIS

Offer bronzy foliage on some species. Fully hardy.

CULTIVATION
C.cheilanthifolia prefers full sun or partial shade and fertile, well-drained soil. May self-seed freely.
C.flexuosa prefers partial shade and moderately fertile, humus-rich, moist but well-drained soil. It is summer dormant.

PROPAGATION
Divide spring flowering species in autumn.

C.cheilanthifolia bears pretty bronze ferny foliage and primrose flowers from early winter to summer. 30cm (12").

C.flexuosa 'Nightshade' bears clusters of purple flowers fading to smoky blue in December to January and later if it is kept cool and moist. The dusky leaves are marked with purple. A seedling found by Bob Brown at his nursery from C.flexuosa 'Pere David'. 25cm (10cm).

C.flexuosa 'Purple Leaf' bears pure blue flowers over reddish-purple leaves from March to May and in autumn. 30cm (12").

C.flexuosa purple seedling has green leaves and purple flowers.

CORYLUS

From northern temperate regions usually in woodland. Hazels offer a good purple form. They are fully hardy.

CULTIVATION
Grow in fertile, well-drained soil in sun for the best colour. Good on chalky soils. Remove any suckers.

PROPAGATION
Sow fresh seed in a seedbed. Layer cultivars in autumn, graft in winter.

C.maxima 'Purpurea' has deep purple foliage especially in full sun, with purple-tinged catkins and fruit husks.

COSMOS

This tuberous-rooted perennial should be known to everyone who loves black plants. Commonly known as Black or Chocolate Cosmos.

CULTIVATION
In mild areas mulch in winter, otherwise lift like a dahlia and keep tubers frost free.

PROPAGATION
Does not come true from seed, root basal cuttings with bottom heat in early spring.

C.atrosanguineus may or may not have a chocolate scent (aided by warm evenings) but it does have delicious velvet-textured, dark-maroon with a dark centre, spoon-shaped flowers. Darker on first opening. Reddish stems and pinnate dark green leaves. Flowers midsummer to autumn. 75cm (30"). One of my favourites and deserves to be widely used.

COTINUS

Offering good purple foliage in some cultivars, these deciduous trees and shrubs offer a good backdrop for smaller plants. Excellent autumn colour and they are fully hardy.

CULTIVATION
Moderately fertile, moist but well-drained soil in full sun for purple leaved forms.

PROPAGATION
Sow seed in a cold frame in autumn. Layer in spring. Root softwood cuttings in summer.

C.coggygria 'Grace' is a tree-like hybrid with large, soft purplish foliage which becomes reddish in autumn. Bears fruiting panicles of purple-pink. 6m (20ft)
C.coggygria 'Notcutt's Variety' bears dark maroon-purple leaves.
C.coggygria 'Royal Purple' has dark red-purple foliage, translucent in sunshine, reddening towards autumn. It is perhaps the best choice with the darkest foliage.
C.coggygria Rubrifolius Group (synonym Foliis Purpureis) has purplish foliage when young which later turns purplish-green or green. Possibly a seed-strain, it is an old form and the parent of many of the modern purple-leaved forms.
C.coggygria Purpureus Group (syn. f purpureus) is purplish only in its inflorescences, the foliage being green, turning orange and red in autumn.
C.coggygria 'Velvet Cloak' has purple foliage which turns reddish purple in autumn.
C.obovatus is a broadly conical shrub or small tree with leaves to 12cm (5") or more. These are pinkish bronze when young turning to brilliant orange, red and purple in autumn. Pinkish-grey fruiting panicles persist into autumn. 10m (30ft).

CRINUM

I have never seen the purple leaved form anywhere except the tropical gardens at Waimea on the island of Oahu, Hawaii, and it took my breath away. Well worth seeking. Frost tender.

CULTIVATION
Plant in spring with the neck of the bulb just above soil level. Under glass, grow in loam-based potting compost with sharp sand and well-rotted manure in full or bright filtered light. Water freely when in growth, keep moist after flowering. Pot on only when absolutely necessary in early spring. Outdoors, grow in deep, fertile, humus-rich, moist but well-drained soil in full sun.

PROPAGATION
Difficult to divide. Sow fresh seed under glass. Takes some years to flower.

Labelled as **C.purpureum** in the tropical garden where I found it, this plant certainly has great presence. A lovely deep shade of purple on this architectural beauty which would make a statement in any garden.

CROCOSMIA

A few cultivars of these cormous perennials from South Africa offer bronzed foliage, which contrasts well with their attractive flowers which are often produced late in the season. Flowers are good for cutting. They are good at the edge of a border, although leaves can be a little untidy. They are fully to frost hardy.

CULTIVATION
Corms should be planted at a depth of 8-10cm (3-4") in spring in moderately fertile, humus-rich, moist but well-drained soil in sun or partial shade.

PROPAGATION
Sow fresh seed in a cold frame. Divide in spring when overcrowded.

C.x crocosmiiflora 'Dusky Maiden' bears brownish orange flowers and has deep bronze leaves.
C.x.crocosmiiflora 'Gerbe d'Or' has brown leaves and apricot flowers and is similar to, but hardier and more vigorous than 'Solfaterre'.
C.x crocosmiiflora 'Solfaterre' is a choice plant for a warm situation near a sunny wall as long as it is not too dry. Pale apricot flowers borne in midsummer contrast with smoky-brown foliage. Mulch well in the first winter. 46cm (18").
C.x crocosmiiflora 'Sultan' has elegant dusky brown leaves and large red flowers from August to October. 75cm (30").

CRYPTOTAENIA

C.japonica f atropurpurea makes a handsome foliage plant with its trifoliate purple leaves with pointed leaflets, up to 7.5cm (3"). Makes a mound on dark stems and is a strong, erect plant. Tip sprays of insignificant flowers can be removed. 46cm (18"). Fast becoming a firm favourite.

DAHLIA

Needing no introduction, new bronzed foliage Dahlias are introduced every year. Flowers are late in the season when many other plants are past their best. Frost tender.

CULTIVATION
Grow in fertile, humus-rich, well-drained soil in full sun. Feed with a high-nitrogen feed once a week in early summer, then a

high-potash feed once a week to promote flowering from midsummer to early autumn. Stake and dead-head as required. Cut back stems after foliage has been blackened by frosts, and lift the tubers. hang upside down to dry. Store frost-free in peat or dry sand in a well-ventilated place. In frost-free areas leave in the ground and protect with a mulch.

PROPAGATION

Sow seed of bedding types in early spring, hardening off before planting out after the last frosts. Take basal shoot cuttings from tubers started into growth under glass in late winter or early spring. It is possible to take many cuttings from one tuber. Tubers can be divided, each with an eye.

D.'Arabian Night' has deep maroon-black flowers with green foliage.

D.'Bednall Beauty' is like the one below but with crimson flowers.

D.'Bishop of Llandaff' is well-known, bearing purple-burgundy foliage and peony- scarlet flowers. It is deservedly popular, but obtain a good one it can be variable.1.m (3ft).

D.'Black Fire' is a small flowered decorative.

D.'Black Monarch' is a decorative giant type with oxblood-red blooms with some black hints, shading to crimson. 1.2m (4ft).

D.'Copper Queen' is a new introduction from New Zealand having deep crimson flowers over deep beetroot foliage. 1.1m (3.5ft).

D.'Crossfield Ebony' is a tiny pompom form with black-red flowers. At least 1m.

D.'Danjo Doc' has impressive blooms of the deepest wine crimson. 1.3m (4ft).

D.'David Howard' is one of the best decorative-types with its dark purplish foliage and double light orange flowers all summer which contrast well. 90cm (3ft).

D.'Ellen Huston' is a superb double flowering orange-scarlet with contrasting dark purple foliage. 30cm (12").

D.'Fascination' has light semi-double pinkish-purple flowers against dark bronze-black foliage. 60cm (2ft).

D.'Fire Mountain' from NZ. has fire red blooms over almost black foliage. (3.5ft).

D.'Grenadier' is an old variety with double scarlet flowers and dark blackish foliage.

D.'Haresbrook' bears large semi-double deep purple flowers over blackish foliage all summer. 60cm (2ft).

D.'Magenta Magic' has bright red stamens surrounded by dark magenta petals, tipped and edged light pink. Attractive purplish-black foliage. 50cm (20").

D.'Midnight Sun' again from N.Z. this time with deep yellow flowers over almost black foliage. 1.1m (3.5ft).

D.'Moonfire' has dark purple foliage with soft yellow-orange and vermillion flowers. Quite distinctive. 60cm (2ft).

D.'Moor Place' is an oustanding wine-red pompon type which is good for exhibition. 1.1m (3.5ft).

D.'Preston Park' has single scarlet flowers and almost black foliage. 45cm (18").

D.'Rip City' has amazing black-red double blooms 15cm across. A giant 1.2-1.8m.

D.'Roxy' bears dark foliage with startling magenta flowers from June to the first frosts. Floriferous. 40cm (16").

D.'Summer Night' is a very dark blackish-crimson flower on a cactus-type.1.2m.

D.'Tally-Ho' is another fine form with desirable purple-black foliage with single flowers of rich vermillion.

D.'Yellow Hammer' has yellow flowers to contrast with its dark, almost black foliage. Bedding type Dahlias available from seed- **D.'Diablo'** bears bright-coloured blooms above deep bronze foliage. **D.'Redskin'** has double flowers,with maroon to bronzy-green foliage. **D.Classic Series** has bronzy foliage and paeony flowers.

DATURA

Rarely available in the U.K., but usually obtainable in the U.S. is a black form which surely must be worth seeking out. Often available as seed. **D.metel black** has dark purple flowers.

DELPHINIUM

Generally, far too well-known to need an introduction, there are three mentioned here, which, however may not be quite dark enough.

CULTIVATION
Grow in fertile soil in full sun, staking and sheltering Pacific Hybrids from strong winds.

PROPAGATION
Sow seed in early spring.

D. Black Knight Group is a Pacific hybrid perennial bearing very dark purple flowers with a black eye. Short-lived perennial and can be variable in colour. It is fully hardy. Over 1.6m (5ft)

D.brunonianum is an upright perennial with hairy stems and deeply lobed leaves. In early summer racemes of hooded, single, short-spurred deep blue to purple flowers are borne with black-purple eyes, black spurs and heavy veining. It is good for a rock garden. 20cm (8").

D.speciosum bears loose spikes of violet and black flowers above hairy leaves. It flowers in late summer, but is tricky in the open garden. Protect well from slugs. 50cm (20").

DIANTHUS

Some lovely dark flowers available here and mostly available from seed too. Select the darkest.

CULTIVATION
Fully hardy Dianthus species and cultivars prefer well-drained, neutral to alkaline soil in full sun. Young border carnations and pinks will appreciate soil enriched with well-rotted manure or garden compost. Take care not to plant too deep.

PROPAGATION
Sow seed of annuals and biennials under glass in early spring, or biennials in situ in autumn. Take cuttings from Dianthus perennials in summer. Layer border carnations after flowering.

D.barbatus Nigrescens Group darkest flowers on green or mahogany foliage.
D.barbatus 'Sooty' is by far the best Sweet William with that rare and stunning combination of densely packed heads of darkest maroon-red, almost black flowers and deepest mahogany foliage to match (darkens as the season progresses). 30cm.
D.Black and White Minstrels Group is a variety which is easily grown from seed. A half hardy annual pink. Blooms from June to the first frosts with a light fragrance. A striking contrast of deep purple, bordering on black and white double flowers. 30cm (12").
D.'Charcoal' has unbelievable charcoal-grey purple flowers with crimson slashes from July-August. Poor shape but an unusual colour. Border carnation.
D. 'King of the Blacks' bears flowers of the very darkest velvety purple-crimson. hardy perennial carnation to 60cm (2ft)

Look out for the beautiful double Sweet Williams being raised, some dark colours are amongst them.

DIERAMA

This is a genus to watch for the exciting development of ever darker cultivars.
D.pulcherrimum 'Blackbird' has deep wine flowers from black buds. 1.5m (4.5ft). A word of caution, many plants in cultivation are not the real thing.
D.'Black Knight' is slightly darker still. 1.2m (4ft).
D.'Midnight Chimes' is hopefully to be released in the near future. It is black with deep magenta flashing.
I am indebted to Gary Dunlop of Ballyrogan Nurseries, N.Ireland for the above descriptions. Gary tells me he has other dark cultivars coming on which are un-named at the present time.

CULTIVATION
Corms should be planted at a depth of 5-7cm (2-3") deep in spring. Grow in a sheltered spot in humus-rich soil which should be well-drained. Water freely during the growing season. Can be grown under glass in frost-prone areas. Established clumps can withstand temperatures to -10°C (14°F).

PROPAGATION
Sow fresh seed in a cold frame. Divide in spring, may take a while to re-establish.

DODONAEA

In this genus of 50-60 evergreen shrubs and small trees from tropical and subtropical areas there is a gem of purple foliage. This tender subject would need to be grown under glass in frost-prone areas, elsewhere it is suitable for a border or as hedging.

CULTIVATION
Under glass, grow in loam-based potting compost in full light. When in growth, water freely and apply a balanced feed monthly. Reduce watering considerably in winter. Top dress or pot on each spring.
Outdoors grow in moderately fertile, moist but well-drained soil in full sun. Pinch out tips of young shoots to encourage bushy growth.

PROPAGATION
Sow seed in spring. Root semi-ripe cuttings with bottom heat in summer.

D.viscosa 'Purpurea' is a vigorous, erect to spreading shrub with foliage strongly suffused purple. Bears pink to reddish brown, or purple capsules from summer to autumn. Tolerates drought and exposure to wind in coastal areas. 1-5m (3-15ft).

DIGITALIS

The darkest Foxglove I have come across is one of chocolate-brown hue.

D.parviflora bears densely packed spikes of chocolate funnels, can be brown-dark orange with purple-brown lips. It is a clump-forming perennial with dark green leaves. Flowers in mid-summer and is fully hardy. 60cm (24").

DRACUNCULUS

D.vulgaris certainly has the right colour in its flower if not the most pleasant aroma. The purple spathe and purple, shining, almost black spadix rise from basal leaves of dark green, marked purple-brown. Plant the frost hardy tubers at a depth of 15cm (6"). Grow in full sun or partial shade and protect with mulch. Do not stand too close! 1.5m (5ft).

ECHEVERIA

Attractive, mainly evergreen succulents make up this genus of around 150 species. Leaves are often tinged red, but there is something a little more than that on offer to those seeking dark plants. They are often found in semi-desert areas and are frost tender.

CULTIVATION

Under glass, grow in cactus compost in full light. Water moderately when in growth, applying a balanced feed monthly. In winter, keep barely moist. Can be placed outdoors in summer.
Outdoors, grow in moderately fertile to poor soil in full sun.

PROPAGATION

Sow fresh seed under glass. Root stem or leaf cuttings in late spring, or separate offsets in spring.

E.affinis has almost black foliage.
E.agavoides 'Metallica' has grey-flushed, irridescent purple fleshy rosettes.
E.'Baron Bold' would be worth seeking for its unusual, crinkled leaves flushed purple, particularly in cold weather.
E.'Black Knight' has thick green leaves which are flushed purple with red flowers.
E.'Black Prince' is a rare black-leaved form with red flowers which is very choice.
E.'Delight' is flushed pinkish-purple especially at the edges of its charming, crinkled leaves.
E.nodulosa has erect stems with whitish rosettes which are heavily marked with purple-red margins.

A number of interesting Echeverias bear foliage which is tinged red, including **E.agavoides**, **E.pulvinata** and **E.secunda**.

EDITHCOLEA

A genus of one or two species of perennial succulents, closely related to the often difficult to grow Caralluma which can have purple stems. One of those very dark flowers that the uninitiated, who think dark plants are sombre, would perhaps call ugly. These frost tender plants are suitable for desert gardens or warm greenhouses.

CULTIVATION

Under glass, grow in loam-based compost with added grit in full light. Water moderately when in growth, applying a balanced feed once a month. Keep almost dry when dormant.
Outdoors, grow in sharply drained, moderately fertile soil in full sun.

PROPAGATION

Sow seed under glass in spring. Root stem cuttings in spring or autumn.

E.grandis is an unusual variable succulent of decumbent or semi-erect habit. Its greyish-green stems bear 'thorns' and a distinguishing feature is that some stems appear to grow spiky crown-like tops. Leaves are scale-like and short-lived. Its large, dark brown flowers to 10-13cm (4-5") across are striped and spotted with creamy yellow and purple centres. They have hairy margins and are borne from summer to early autumn. 30cm (12"). Minimum temperature 16°C (61°F).
Rare and worth seeking. Doug and Vivi Rowland tell me this is very rare in cultivation and difficult to cultivate in the U.K. being very cold tender. Seeds, when available germinate quickly and easily. Once imported from its native Africa (Kenya, Somalia) but this has ceased as it became endangered.

ELATOSTEMA

You may find these plants still named under the synonym of Pellionia. Leaves are heavily marked with silver or bronze and can appear 'black'. Foliage is very attractive, but stems can be brittle. Frost tender.

CULTIVATION
Under glass, grow in loamless compost in bright, but indirect light. Water freely when in growth and apply a balanced feed every month. In winter, water moderately. Outdoors, grow in humus-rich, fertile soil in deep shade. Minimum temperature required 13°C (55°F).

PROPAGATION
Root cuttings any time of the year.

E. repens has fleshy greenish, pink stems. Its wavy-margined dark, blackish green leaves are attractively marked grey and pale green and are often bronze-flushed. On the undersides, they are often tinged pink with purple margins. Makes good ground cover or is suitable for hanging baskets. 10cm (4").
E.repens v pulchrum has purple-tinged stems with dark green leaves bearing very dark mid-ribs and veins and tinged purple on the undersides. Its trailing habit is suitable for hanging baskets. 8cm (3").

EPISCIA

Flame Violets are evergreen perennials from tropical forests of creeping habit. The leaves are often puckered and many are bronze-coloured. Attractive flowers are produced from spring to autumn. Grow these frost tender plants in hanging baskets or in a warm greenhouse or conservatory.

CULTIVATION
Under glass grow in loamless compost with added vermiculite. Best in bright, filtered light with high humidity. In growth, water moderately, apply a quarter-strength balanced feed at each watering. Keep only just moist in winter. Outdoors, grow in fertile, humus-rich, moist but well-drained soil in partial shade. Minimum temperature 15°C (59°F).

PROPAGATION
Surface sow fresh seed under glass in early spring. Divide or separate plantlets or root stem cuttings with bottom heat in early or midsummer.

E.cupreata is variable but very attractive, especially in its darkest forms where the blistered surfaces of the leaves appear blackish. A mat-forming perennial with toothed, deep copper-green leaves which are purple on the underside. Red and yellow flowers are sometimes spotted purple in the throats. 15cm (6").
E.cupreata 'Acajou' has dark tan leaves, netted with silvery green. Produces orange-red flowers.
E.cupreata 'Mosaica' has the darkest, almost black leaves with a sheen.
E.lilacina has copper-green leaves with purple undersides, bears white flowers with lavender-blue throats.
E.lilacina 'Cuprea' as above but with lavender-blue flowers with white centres.

EUCOMIS

E.'Sparkling Burgundy' is a selected form with dramatic, strap-like purple foliage forming dark burgundy rosettes to 60cm (2ft) wide, best in full sun. A tall stalk arises in late summer, carrying miniature purple pineapples. Easy to grow and tolerant. In cooler climates, grow in a container and give protection in winter.

EUPATORIUM

The herbaceous Eupatoriums can look coarse if not well sited. They are best suited to a large pondside or a large border in retentive soil. They associate well with the larger grasses. Until recently they offered purple tinged foliage, but there have been new introductions which offer that little bit extra. The ones described here are fully hardy and flower late in the season.

CULTIVATION
Grow in retentive soil in moist sun or partial shade.

PROPAGATION
Sow seed in a cold frame in spring. Divide in spring.

E.purpureum subspecies maculatum 'Atropurpureum' is an herbaceous, clump-forming perennial which has darker stems than the species and bright rose-purple flowers on slightly shorter stems. Slightly lime shy. 150cm (4.5ft).

E.album 'Braunlaub' bears brown-flushed young leaves and brown flowers.

E.rugosum 'Chocolate' is proving very popular with its lovely dark bronze foliage and white plates of blooms late in the year. 120-150cm (4-5ft). Colours best in sun, although will tolerate dry shade. Has also been marketed mistakenly under the name 'Brunette'. I have also noticed one catalogue describing the flower colour as pink.

The species **E.purpureum** also offers variable purple-tinged foliage, and stems marked and blotched with purple. Flowers are purple-pink.

EUPHORBIA

A varied and large genus of over 2000 species which offers some very interesting plants. The ones described here are fully hardy.

CULTIVATION
Moist, humus-rich soil in dappled shade. E.dulcis will tolerate drier soil. Please note, sap is irritant.

PROPAGATION
Sow fresh seed of hardy perennials in a cold frame, or sow in spring. Divide in early spring, or take basal cuttings in spring or early summer. Cut surfaces can be dipped in charcoal or lukewarm water to prevent bleeding. Please wear long protective gloves.

E.amygdaloides 'Purpurea' (syn. 'Rubra') is a very attractive, superb form of the native Wood Spurge. Maroon stems carry dark evergreen leaves, while the new shoots are vividly tinted beetroot-red, followed by bright yellow-green flower bracts. 80cm (32").

E. characias ssp characias 'Perry's Winter Blusher' gives a marvellous winter show and has flowers and stems flushed red. 1-1.5m (3ft or more).

E.dulcis bears dark or bronze-green leaves with greenish-yellow flowers. In autumn, stems turn red and leaves turn red, gold and orange. Self seeds freely. 30cm (1ft).

E.dulcis 'Chameleon' would be my choice for the garden bearing deep purple foliage which is retained if positioned in full sun. It bears purple-tinted greenish yellow flowers. 30cm (1ft).

E.'Purple Preference' has leaves flushed purple with gingery flowers in spring. 75cm (2.5ft).

E.polychroma 'Candy' and E.'Redwing' have purple-tinted foliage.

FAGUS

Must surely be the most well-known purple foliage tree. Has always been my favourite tree, which perhaps in part explains my passion for these dark plants. Makes a superb specimen tree. Fully hardy and F.sylvatica does not need long hot summers like the other species to do well.

CULTIVATION

Very tolerant of a wide range of soils including chalk. Prefers well-drained soil in full sun or partial shade. Purple-leaved beeches are best positioned in full sun, when their exquisite colour will dazzle. In late summer or early spring remove wayward or crossing shoots to maintain a good framework.

PROPAGATION

Sow seed in a seedbed in autumn. Alternatively, stratify seed and sow in spring. Cultivars can be grafted in midwinter.

F.sylvatica 'Ansorgei' is a shrubby hybrid between F.sylvatica purple-leaved and a fern-leaved form producing brownish purple, lanceolate, almost entire leaves.

F.sylvatica Atropurpurea Group, can be rather variable in purple hue, turning coppery in autumn.

F.syvatica 'Black Swan' bears dark purple foliage which holds its colour well, with a handsome weeping habit.

F.sylvatica 'Brocklesbury' has deep purple leaves which are larger than the norm. There is an example at Kew.

F.syvatica Cuprea Group is used to denote trees of a paler purple leaf colour, the copper form.

F.sylvatica 'Dawyck Purple' is narrowly upright with deep purple foliage. 20m (70ft) with a spread of just 5m (15ft).

F.sylvatica 'Purple Fountain' is a seedling of F.s. 'Purpurea Pendula' raised in Holland. It makes a narrowly upright tree with purple leaves and weeping branches.

F.sylvatica 'Purpurea Pendula' the weeping purple beech has stiff, pendulous branches which bear deep purple-blackish leaves.

F.sylvatica 'Purpurea Nana' is, as its name suggests, a dwarf form, slow-growing and eventually making a mushroom-shaped bush.

F.sylvatica 'Purpurea Tricolor' has purple leaves unusually marked at the edges with pink or pinkish white. The markings are not always constant.

F.sylvatica 'Riversii' has very dark purple leaves, perhaps the darkest. An old cultivar, listed since the 1870's.

F.sylvatica 'Rohanii' differs in that its reddish brownish-purple leaves are attractively and deeply cut. It is known as the fern leaf beech. This makes a beautiful, slow-growing tree. Raised in 1888 from seed, it has been in commerce since 1908.

F.sylvatica 'Swat Magret' was raised in Germany, having very dark leaves which retain their colour until late summer.

FRITILLARIA

Sumptuous dark flowers are to be found amongst the 100 or so species of this genus of bulbous perennials. They are fully to frost hardy depending on the species.

CULTIVATION
Since Fritillarias come from many different habitats around the world, their cultural requirements differ. Handle fragile bulbs with care.

PROPAGATION
Sow seed in autumn in a cold frame, exposing to winter cold. Should germinate in spring when they can be transferred to a cold greenhouse. Grow on small species in their container for two years before planting out.
Divide offsets and sow basal bulbils in late summer.

F.biflora is known as the black fritillary. It offers bell-shaped, brownish flowers tinged purple to black and flushed green. It is intolerant of wet and is perhaps best grown in a bulb frame even though it is hardy. 15-30cm (6-12").
F.biflora 'Martha Roderick' is the best form producing deep red-purple flowers with two thirds of the outer tepals being white or creamish chocolate brown.
Far darker and possibly "Black Queen" of the species is **F.camschatcensis**, the black sarana. It can be variable and produce green or yellow flowers. When you have a good form, the bells produced in early summer are unbelievably black. Smooth and silky on the outside and corrugated on the inside. Needs rich leaf-mould and grows best in areas with cool, damp summers as it is a woodland species.45cm (18"). F.camschatcensis black is sometimes offered, should be consistent. Better still,

there are two cultivars to look out for.
F.camschatcensis 'Amur' and 'Tomari' are really black, my American friend obtained hers from a Latvian Nursery. 'Amur' is described by the nursery as being brownish-black and 'Tomari' as bluish black. Grow in full sun.
F.graeca has deep green flowers, almost wholly chequered with brownish purple. It is intolerant of wet, especially when dormant. 5-20cm (2-8").
F.latifolia displays broadly bell-shaped, dark maroon to purplish flowers. Again, it is intolerant of wet. 10-20cm (4-8").
The delightful and very well-known **F.meleagris**, the snake's head fritillary, may be dark enough for some, as a good form will bear dark purple broadly bell-shaped flowers with strong pinkish tessellation. Can be quite robust and is excellent for naturalising in grass. Flowers in April. 5-8cm (2-3").
F.michailovskyi is a gem for the bulb frame or alpine house with its shining damson-coloured flowers, tipped with yellow or yellowish-green. 10-20cm (4-8").
F.persica bears greenish-brown to deep purple flowers. It is a robust species with sturdy, upright stems. Suitable for a sunny border or rock garden in full sun. 1m (3ft).
F.persica 'Adiyaman' is taller and more free-flowering than the species, bearing brown-purple flowers. 1.5m (5ft).
F.pyrenaica which has been known under the synonym of F.nigra h., has deep brownish-purple flowers, occasionally yellow, which are strongly tessellated. They are yellow-green on the inside. Grow as for F.persica. 45cm (18").
F.sewerzowii is a variable species which bears greenish-yellow to vivid purple flowers, each yellow within. Intolerant of wet. 30cm (12").
F.uva-vulpis is choice almost wholly greyish-purple with bright gold tips. Found growing in cornfields in its native Turkey, Iran and Iraq. 20cm (8").

FUCHSIA

Unfortunately, the colour black is very subjective and I found the Fuchsias I purchased to be rather disappointing in their shade of purple, but mostly because they had black in their name.

F. 'Alice Hoffman' has purple-tinged, bronze-green foliage to compliment the small, semi-double flowers with rose-pink tubes and sepals and white corollas which are veined rose-pink. May not be frost hardy in some areas. 45-60cm (18-24").

F.'Black Beauty' and **F.'Black Prince'** although they are perfectly good flowers, are not ones I would describe as black. Mr.Gilbert of Silverdale Fuchsias assures me that 30 years ago if you had purchased 'Black Prince' you would have found it very near black, but it has sadly declined in colour in cultivation.

F.'Lady Boothby' is hardy and very dark. There are also two described as dark aubergine **F.'Lechlade Magician'** and **F.'Whiteknights Amethyst'** .

F.'Zulu Girl' from New Zealand is also very dark .

F.triphylla has leaves purple on the underside and the two cultivars **'Thalia'** and **'Gartenmeister Bonstedt'** have velvety bronze-red leaves.

GAURA

G.lindheimerei is a beautiful plant of incredible grace, especially 'The Bride' one of my favourite white flowers, so I am pleased that there is a plant with apparently darker foliage.

G.lindheimeri 'Siskiyou Pink' has dark greenish-purple or bronze foliage with attractive spikes of pink flowers all summer. 60cm (2ft).

GERANIUM

Hardy Geraniums are superb herbaceous perennials which look good in the border and can be used to effect beneath roses or as groundcover. Found in all but very wet habitats in temperate regions throughout the world. Attractive leaves, sometimes dark or blotched and dark flowers have been produced, and a second flush is often possible on some when cut back after flowering. Most are fully hardy and easy to grow.

CULTIVATION
Larger species and hybrids can be grown in any moderately fertile soil, in full sun or partial shade. Small species require sharply-drained soil in full sun.

PROPAGATION
Sow fresh seed outdoors as soon as possible or sow in spring.

G.'Anne Thomson' is an Alan Bremner hybrid with golden-green foliage having dusky-purple flowers with black centres from June to frost. Sun to partial shade.

G.'Bertie Crug' has attractive dark bronze foliage and forms low mounds studded with deep pink flowers. This is a charming prostrate creeper.

G.'Black Ice' is a cross between G.traversii and G.sessiliflorum ssp novae-zelandiae 'Nigricans' which produces dark grey-brown leaves and white flowers. (A.Bremner hybrid). Prefers full sun and well-drained soil.

G.'Crug's Darkest' also known as Crug's Dark Delight has the darkest silky leaves with pink flowers just above the foliage.

G.'Crug Strain' is a low growing perennial bearing dark foliage and flowers from pink to white. The Crugs are constantly making selections from this strain.

G.'Dusky Crug' was a chance seedling producing low-growing, large roundish, velvety brown leaves.

G.'Elizabeth Wood' also makes low mounds with pink flowers and has slightly bronzed leaves.

G.'Kate' has dark bronze foliage, with extending flower stems showing its Folkard parentage and pink flowers. 20cm

G.'Libretto' is another Alan Bremner hybrid wih dark foliage and white flowers. 20cm (8").

G.'Orkney Pink' is also from Alan Bremner with dark bronzy-grey foliage and extending flower stems, bearing purple-pink flowers from June to frost.

G.phaeum , the dusky cranesbill, is clump-forming with soft-green basal leaves, often with purplish-brown marks. In late spring to early summer, it bears pendent, white-centred, deep purple-black or maroon flowers, occasionally light or violet blue, rarely white on lax stems. 80cm (32").

G.phaeum 'Chocolate Chip' is an American form claiming the darkest flowers, my American friend who has this says she has seen darker flowers on others.

G.phaeum 'Mourning Widow' is a strong grower in shade with dark purple-black, silk-textured blooms in early summer. 80cm (32").

G.phaeum 'Samobor' is valued for its outstanding large leaves, handsomely marked with a chocolate blotch with waxy, midnight-purple flowers. Give good soil for the best effect. 60cm (2ft).

G.pratense Midnight Reiter Strain has purple tinged foliage. 'Night Reiter' has black-burgundy leaves. 'Victor Reiter' has deep red leaves which are black-red when young.

G.pratense 'Purple Haze' is a dark-leaved form available as seed from Ray Brown of Plant World. A superb plant, selected leaf colours now vary from mahogany-bronze to deepest, darkest beetroot. Can be variable in height and flower colour.

G.'Rosie Crug' though not as dark as some, has pewtery grey foliage.

G.'Sea Spray' an Alan Bremner hybrid has bronze foliage and a succession of small pink flowers until the first frosts.

G.sessiliflorum 'Rubrum' with darkest red mahogany foliage studded with contrasting white flowers all summer.

G.sessiliflorum ssp novae-zelandiae 'Nigricans' has tufts of olive-bronze basal divided leaves. In summer it bears greyish-white flowers.

G.sessiliflorum ssp novae-zelandiae 'Porter's Pass' has prostrate chestnut-brown leaves, contrasting with pink flowers on this tiny plant which the slugs just love to eat to extinction in my garden. 5cm (2"). A real little gem.

G.sinense has astonishing red beaks protuding from the darkest deepest maroon-purple, almost black reflexed petals. One of the darkest flowered Geraniums.

G.'Strawberry Frost' forms a small clump of rich purple-brown leaves (silvery brown) and masses of pretty pink flowers all summer. Requires a sunny, well-drained position.

G.'Welsh Guiness' is an Alan Bremner hybrid. A prostrate and creeping plant weaving a dark, glossy mat studded with many small white flowers which give perfect contrast to the foliage.

G.x monacense 'Muldoon' is a clump-forming perennial with dark purple, reflexed flowers and dark-blotched variegated leaves. Best in part to full shade in well-drained soil. The Crugs give the same description for G.x monacense 'Variegatum'.

G.x oxonianum 'Buttercup' , 'Fran's Star','Jester' and 'Walter's Gift' as well as G. reflexum have distinctive dark markings on the leaves. G. x monacense has leaves heavily spotted with chocolate. G.phaeum 'Calligrapher' has dark contour lines.

GLADIOLUS

Now who could resist a black Gladiolus? Not easy to find, but they are out there.

CULTIVATION
Grow in fertile, well-drained soil in full sun. Corms should be planted at a depth of 10-16cm (4-6") deep in spring. A bed of sharp sand will aid drainage. Lift when the leaves turn yellowish and snap from the corm, store frost-free.

PROPAGATION
Sow seed of species in containers in spring. Separate cormlets when dormant.

G.'Black Lash' is probably the easiest to find. It is a small-flowered form with flowers of black-rose. Bred by Ed Frederick and introduced in 1976. It still wins at Gladiolus Shows today.

Most black- red or black-rose Gladiolus are bred in the Czech Republic or America. Large-flowered Gladiolus to look out for include **'Black Dancer'**, **'Blackwood'**, **'Dark Victory'**. Of the medium -flowered types you could try **'Burgundy Queen'**. In the small-flowered types are **'Dark Mystery'** and **'Dave's Memory'**.

Bill Murray of Edinburgh has bred some dark-flowered primulinus type Gladiolus including **'Brush Strokes'** which is a black-rose with grey dusting.
Of the species, the tender **G.callianthus** bears strongly-scentedwhite flowers marked with purple in the throat. Not at all like the hybrids above.
G.papilio Purpureoauratus Group is another attractive species not quite as tender as the above. Flowers can vary from cream to yellow, but all are heavily marked with purple.

GLEDITSIA

The flowers of Gleditsias are inconspicuous and are grown for their foliage and interesting seedpods. One offers good bronze and purple colour. They are fully hardy.

CULTIVATION
Any fertile well-drained soil will suit them, in full sun. Protect from frost damage when young.

PROPAGATION
Scarify seed and sow in an open frame in autumn. Bud cultivars in summer or graft in late winter.

G.triacanthos is a spiny, deciduous tree. Pendent, sickle-shaped seedpods to 45cm (18") long are borne in autumn. **'Rubylace'** has wonderful dark-bronze red-purple leaves when young turning to dark bronze-green by midsummer.

GYNURA

From the 50 species which make up this genus, there is something of interest in purple foliage. Frost tender.

CULTIVATION
In frost prone areas, grow under glass in loam-based compost in bright, filtered light. Pot on or top dress in spring. In growth, water freely, apply a balanced feed monthly. Pinch out tips. Outdoors, grow in fertile, moist but well-drained soil in partial shade.

PROPAGATION
Root softwood cuttings in late spring or semi-ripe in summer, with bottom heat.

G.aurantiaca 'Purple Passion' is trailing or semi-twining with a hint of purple flush.

HALORAGIS

New Zealand plants, related to Gunneras give a bronze form which is quite eye-catching and certainly not something everyone will have. Half hardy.

CULTIVATION
Will prefer well-drained, fertile soil. In frost prone areas, grow under glass. Can be placed outdoors in summer.

PROPAGATION
Relatively easy from seed. Sow under glass in spring.

H.'Wellington Bronze' is an attractive foliage form of H.erecta. The bronzed leaves add colour to the border both before and after the main flush of garden flowers. Foliage has attractively serrated margins. Bears spikes of many small, almost insignificant greenish-yellow flowers. An erect, branching half-hardy perennial which deserves to be more widely used. 60cm (2ft). One seed firm markets this as 'Melton Bronze', although it appears to be even more compact at 30cm (12"), and is promoted for use in baskets and containers.

HEBE

Grown for both foliage and flowers, the former offers purple tinges, and the latter some exciting shades of purple but not really dark enough for inclusion here. They are fully hardy to half hardy.

CULTIVATION
Grow in poor or moderately fertile, moist but well-drained soil. Neutral to slightly alkaline soil suits them best in sun or partial shade.

PROPAGATION
Seed is not normally recommended and Hebes do hybridise freely. Semi-ripe cuttings are easy to root in late summer or autumn with bottom heat.

H.'Amy' has elegant large, purple-bronze leaves when young and colours well in winter, with purple flowers. Needs some shelter in colder areas. 75-120cm (30-45").
H.'Autumn Glory' has green leaves, purplish especially when young and dark chunky violet flowers in June to September. 45cm (18").
H.'Fairfieldii' is an upright shrub, with coarsely toothed, glossy mid-dark green, red-margined leaves, having lavender-violet flowers. Frost hardy.
H.'Great Orme' has dark purple shoots.
H.'Hinderwell' was bred in the north and has sumptuous, red-purple leaves and deep violet flowers. 60cm (24").
H.'La Seduisante' has dark purple shoots and green leaves which are purple on the underside. It bears medium-sized, dark purple-red flowers.
H.'Midsummer Beauty' has bright green leaves, red-purple beneath when young.
H.'Mrs Winder' has purplish-brown shoots and leaves of dark-red purple when young.

HEDERA

Not as popular as the green forms are the Ivies which offer darker foliage. I prefer them to the green, they make an excellent backdrop and look more dramatic than their counterparts when covering a wall, especially in winter. Fully hardy.

CULTIVATION
Ivies can tolerate a wide range of conditions. Fertile, moist but well-drained soil suits them best, preferably humus-rich and alkaline.

PROPAGATION
In summer, root semi-ripe cuttings of juvenile form to obtain plants of trailing habit.

H.helix 'Atropurpurea' (synonym 'Purpurea'), the purple-leaved Ivy, has large, 5-lobed blackish green leaves which gradually turn deep purple in cold weather. Foliage is strongly veined green and very attractive. Excellent on a wall. 8m (25ft).

H.helix 'Donerailensis' bears small leaves which turn brownish-purple in winter. Best grown in a pot with its roots restricted to retain its character.

H.helix 'Glymii' differs from the above in that it has medium-sized entire to 3-lobed, glossy dark green leaves which turn deep red-purple in cold weather. Each leaf is curled or twisted which increases as the season progresses. Excellent on a wall or for use in a chimney pot. Not too robust. 2m (6ft).

H.hibernica 'Gracilis' has wiry stems of a warm purple hue with dull green leaves becoming bronzed in autumn.

HELIANTHUS

Not all Sunflowers are yellow. Dark bronze shades and deep velvet reds have been recently introduced.

CULTIVATION
They thrive in moist soil with plenty of feed if you want to grow the giant, single-headed types. The giant sunflower is still only available in yellow. Position in full sun against a warm wall.

PROPAGATION
Easy from seed, if the birds do not get to it first, can be started indoors, and are best singly in pots.

H.'Chianti' is a striking flower of deep red and almost purple-black centre, shading along the petals from black to red. 1.8m (5ft).

H.'Prado Red' is a multi-flowered type with up to 20 flowers on short stems. They are quick to bloom and almost pollen-free. The stunning flowers are a very deep, uniform red, with a yellow band around the centre which enhances the colour perfectly. There is a yellow counterpart. 1.3-1.8m (4-5ft).

H.'Velvet Queen' is a deep velvet-red to copper. Will appear darker if planted with lighter subjects of pale yellow or white. 1.8m (5ft).

HELLEBORUS

Some of my favourite flowers are found in this genus and in the species H.orientalis, the hybrids do offer some very dark, near black beauties, with purple or blue undertones. The ones here are all fully hardy.

CULTIVATION
A range of moist, fertile, humus rich soils will be tolerated.

PROPAGATION
Sow fresh seed in a coldframe. Divide after flowering.

H.orientalis hybrids are available in colour selections such as purple and black. Helen Ballard's are considered the best blacks, having large rich dark-purple flowers. There are many dark, blue-black seedlings from this strain. Many years ago there was a German hybrid named **H. 'Black Knight'** but I do not think it is available these days. There is a **H.'Little Black'** and a nearly black available at the time of writing. There is also a single black with make you stop and stare new purple foliage. In the U.S. you might look out for **H.'Birkin's Black'. H.'Smokey Blue'** offers seedlings from the Blackthorn strain. **H.'Pluto'** is an intriguing colour being purple on the outer petals and purple with a green tint within.
H. orientalis 'Purpurascens' bears blooms of dusky purple.
H.purpurascens has leathery, basal mid-green leaves to 27cm (11"). Pendent, cup-shaped flowers of purplish or slate-grey, often flushed pink or purple are borne before the leaves make their appearance. 5-30cm (2-12").
The specific epithet in the species H.niger refers to the black roots of the plant. Its leaves are green and its flowers are white.

HEMEROCALLIS

Fine flowers they are, but I cannot help thinking that some described here have been wrongly named. If you are expecting them to be black, as the names suggest, you are probably going to be disappointed. Mostly fully hardy, and these dark colours tend to be intolerant of full sun and rainfall.

CULTIVATION
Grow in fertile, moist but well-drained soil. Mulch in late autumn or spring. From spring to when the buds appear, water freely and apply a balanced feed every 2 weeks.

PROPAGATION
Sow seed in a cold frame in autumn or spring. Seed from hybrids and cultivars does not come true. Divide every 2-3 years.

H.'Black Falcon' is a plum-purple.
H.'Black Knight' purple from darker buds. Flowers appear June-August. 90cm (3ft approx).
H.'Black Magic' has very dark plum-purple flowers 10cm (4") across from dark buds. 60cm (2ft).
H.'Night Beacon' is a deep purple-brown, with a large green eye. 45cm (18").
H.'Purple Rain' is a deepish burgundy purple. 40cm (16").
H.'So Excited' is a deep red with blackish tones.
H.'Starling' is a red-black daylily with a bright gold reverse and medium-sized flowers. Colours better out of full sun, midday shade perhaps. 1m (3ft).
H.'Super Purple' has very dark maroon-purple flowers 14cm (5.5"). The throats are lime-green and yellow. 65cm (26"). Not quite fully hardy, but does have the bonus of an extended flowering period.

HEMIGRAPHIS

Grown for their colourful, attractively toothed or scalloped leaves which make useful ground cover in warmer climates or can be used in conservatories in colder climes, or even as unusual basket plants, where the undersides of the leaves may show to advantage. Frost tender. You may find these plants from woodland margins of tropical Asia difficult to obtain.

CULTIVATION
Under glass, grow in bright filtered light in loamless or loam-based compost. They require moderate to high humidity. Water freely when in growth and apply a balanced feed monthly. Keep moist in winter. Outdoors, grow in any fertile soil moist but well-drained in partial shade. Shelter from strong winds. Minimum temperature 10°C (50°F).

PROPAGATION
Root softwood or stem-tip cuttings in summer or autumn. Separate rooted stems in spring.

H.alternata (syn. H.colorata) is also known as red flame ivy for the undersides of its attractive leaves to 9cm (3.5") long which are a silvery-grey on the surface. White flowers are borne from spring to summer.
H.'Exotica' is known as the purple waffle plant. This compact, evergreen perennial produces purplish-green leaves to 9cm (3.5") long, puckered between the veins with a purple sheen and are deep-red on the underside. White flowers.
H.repanda has slender maroon-red stems which root down freely. The narrow leaves to 5cm (2") long are red-flushed greyish-green, shading to purple above and dark purple beneath. White flowers.

HERMODACTYLUS

This handsome plant is not the easiest to grow well, but worth the effort. Found on dry, rocky slopes in S.Europe to N.Africa and Israel and Turkey, it needs long hot, dry summers to bake the tubers. Fully hardy.

CULTIVATION
Tubers should be planted at a depth of 10cm (4") in autumn. Choose moderately fertile, sharply drained, alkaline soil in full sun. Dislikes excessive summer rain. Position at the base of a warm, sunny wall. In frost-prone areas, although hardy, the early flowers may be prone to frost, it can be grown under the protection of a bulb frame. In warmer areas it can be naturalised in grass.

PROPAGATION
Divide as soon as the leaves die back.

H.tuberosus, the widow iris is a perennial which slowly forms clumps. The delightful flowers have a most unusual colouring. Some describe the green as glass-green (Beth Chatto) others as jade-green (Avon Bulbs). The greenish-yellow flowers are 5cm (2") across with wondrous velvety blackish-brown outer segments borne in spring. In addition, these extraordinary flowers exude a sweet perfume. The leaves are not unattractive, being linear bluish or greyish-green. They die back in early summer. 20-40cm (8-16").

A delightful flower, not the easiest to grow, but given the right conditions and given time to become established in a hot, sunny spot, you may well be rewarded.

HEUCHERA

This is one genus, that with recent developments, many from Dan Heims in the USA, now offers an outstanding number of purple-leaved hybrids, some of which come remarkably true from seed. They make excellent ground cover. Bees are attracted to the flowers. Fully hardy to frost hardy.

CULTIVATION
Grow in fertile, moist but well-drained soil in sun or partial shade. The woody rootstock can have a tendency to push up and it is best to mulch well.

PROPAGATION
Sow seed in a cold frame in spring and select the best purple foliage. Divide in autumn.

H.'Black Velvet' has dark red leaves.
H.'Beauty Colour' bears wonderful dark, almost black leaves which are overnetted with green and silver.
H.'Cascade Dawn' produces a mound of huge reddish-purple leaves marbled with pewter grey.
H.'Chocolate Ruffles' has luxuriant deep chocolate-purple foliage with nicely scalloped, ruffled edges. 50cm (20").
H.'Eden's Mystery' pushes forth dark, shiny purple leaves which become glossy silver with age. Good, strong young colouring. Has creamy-white flowers. 25cm (10").
H.'Emperor's Cloak' has wondrous puckered, folded and pleated foliage in shades from beetroot to deep purple which appear almost transparent in the sun. From the mound of colourful leaves arise thin stems carrying fluffy white flowers to form the perfect contrast. Sensational.
H. micrantha v diversifolia 'Palace Purple' can be variable from seed, but you will at least get some good deep foliage to select. Overlapping heart-shaped leaves are dark bronze reddish-purple on the surface and lighter on the underside. Faint puckering between the veins accentuates the sheen. Dark wiry stems carry feathery heads of tiny white flowers held well above the foliage. 46cm (18").
H.'Persian Carpet' brings forth purple-red leaves marbled pinkish-grey.
H.'Pewter Veil' has scalloped purple and silver foliage which is fairly light and will make a good contrast to paler plants, maroon flowers. 60cm (2ft).
H.'Plum Puddin' bears foliage of a deep, shiny plum-burgundy purple with silver markings and maroon flowers. 60cm (2ft).
H.'Purple Petticoats' has heavily ruffled leaves of deep maroon. 30cm (12").
H.'Rachel' is a real dark beauty.
H.'Stormy Seas' has attractive, crinkled foliage netted with silver. 30cm (1ft).
H.'Velvet Night' bears dark maroon to black leaves with metallic purple overlays. 30cm (12").
Brown, bronze or maroon foliage is also offered by H.'Can Can', H.'Cappuchino', H.'Cherries Jubilee' , H.'Petite Marlberg', H.'Smoky Rose' and H.villosa 'Biddulph Brown'.

X HEUCHERELLA

A cross between Heuchera and Tiarella. Prefers slightly acid soil. Fully hardy.

x H.'Quicksilver' has metallic purple foliage with bronze veining and bears pink and white flowers from May to July. 30cm.
x H. 'Silver Streak' has paler purple foliage overlaid with silver white and bears white and lavender pink flowers in April to July. 30cm (1ft).

HIBISCUS

Offering such exotic flowers, it is a delight to see the combination of coppery purple foliage too. The species below is frost tender.

CULTIVATION

Under glass, grow in loamless or loam-based compost in bright, filtered light. Requires moderate humidity and good ventilation. When in growth, water freely and apply a balanced feed monthly. Water sparingly in winter.

Where there is no danger of frost, grow outdoors in humus-rich, moist but well-drained, neutral to slightly alkaline soil in full sun.

PROPAGATION

Sow seed under glass in spring. Divide perennials in spring. Root greenwood cuttings of shrubs, or semi-ripe cuttings in summer. Layering can take place in spring or summer.

H.acetosella 'Coppertone' syn 'Red Shield' is a short-lived perennial which needs to be grown under glass in frost-prone areas or can be grown as an annual. The leaves of the species are often flushed red, but 'Coppertone' has broadly ovate, usually deeply lobed leaves of a brilliant maroon-purple. Together with its 5cm (2") across flowers of old rose this is one plant which will delight whether you choose to grow it inside or out. It will flower indoors.

HOYA

Always interesting flowers which you would not want to miss, no matter what their colour. So, we are very lucky that there is a very dark red flower to suit our quest for dark plants. Frost tender species.

CULTIVATION

Require an open, free-draining medium to really flourish. Under glass, grow in loam-based potting compost, with equal parts of added leaf mould, sharp sand, pulverised bark and charcoal. Not at all fussy plants! Position in indirect or bright, filtered light. Need moderate to high humidity. When in growth, water freely and apply a balanced feed monthly. Keep moist in winter.

PROPAGATION

Sow seed under glass in spring. Root semi-ripe cuttings with bottom heat in late summer. Layer in spring or summer.

H.macgillivrayi is a strong-growing, twining climber with thick stems, and rigid, thick fleshy leaves of a lustrous dark green. These are often tinted red-purple when young. From spring to summer, cup-shaped flowers are borne, being 4-8cm (1.5-3") across. Their colour can be anything from red, red-purple, purple or brownish-red to dark-maroon near black. Coronas can also be dark red or occasionally white. See it in flower before you buy. 5-8m (15-25ft). Minimum temperature 7°C (45°F).

H.purpureofusca bears umbels of scented deep maroon flowers.

Other species have dark coronas, including **H.cinnamonifolia** (dark purple) and **H.pauciflora** (dark red) .

HUERNIA

Huernias are curious frost-tender perennial succulents from hilly, semi-desert areas with a faintly unpleasant scent. The flowers are interesting and quite beautiful.

CULTIVATION
Under glass, grow in standard cactus compost with added leaf mould in bright, filtered or indirect light. Provide low humidity. Water moderately in growth, applying a half-strength, high nitrogen feed monthly. Keep virtually dry in winter. Outdoors, grow in poor to moderately fertile soil. Sandy, sharply drained soil is best with sharp sand and leaf mould incorporated when planting. Grow in dappled shade or in full sun with midday shade. Dislike excessive winter wet.

PROPAGATION
Sow seed under glass in spring. Root cuttings of stem sections in spring or summer.

H.macrocarpa v arabica is a handsome species with its flowers of deep maroon purple with white hairs. Borne in early autumn,they are 1cm across. 10cm (4"). Minimum temperature 11°C (52°F).
H.oculata bears flowers of almost blackish-red and a pure white centre.
H.schneiderana has bell-shaped flowers, brownish on the outer surface and velvety, deep purple inside, the margins pinkish and edged with maroon.
H.striata bears greenish or maroon flowers on the outside, yellow on the inside, the whole being marked irregularly with brownish-maroon bands.
H.zebrina has flowers to 3.5cm across of greenish yellow, marked with maroon and a very deep maroon centre. Grows to 8cm.

HYDRANGEA

The best of the Hydrangeas to my eye and one that fortunately offers some winter colour is **H.quercifolia**. Its lobed mid-green leaves turn a good bronze-purple in autumn. It is fully hardy and flowers from midsummer to autumn. Sterile flowers become pink-tinged with age. 2m(6ft).
H.'Preziosa' may also be of interest with its reddish-brown foliage.

CULTIVATION
Moist but well-drained moderately fertile, humus-rich soil in full sun or partial shade with shelter from cold winds.

PROPAGATION
Sow seed in a cold frame in spring. Root softwood cuttings in early summer, or hardwood cuttings in winter.

HYPERICUM

Just one to mention here that has foliage flushed purple, although some leaves may remain green. Fully hardy.

CULTIVATION
Grow in moderately fertile moist but sharply drained soil. Position in full sun or partial shade.

PROPAGATION
Greenwood or semi-ripe cuttings in summer.

H.androsaemum 'Albury Purple' is a deciduous shrub with erect branches and broadly ovate to oblong leaves which are flushed purple. The cupped yellow flowers to 2cm across are borne in midsummer. The red, spherical berry like fruit which follows ripens to black. 75cm.

IRIS

This genus of over 300 species is split into groups. As such their individual cultivation requirements differ. They are mostly hardy, but some thrive only in specific conditions. Most need long, hot summers to do really well.

GENERAL CULTIVATION

Plant in late summer and early autumn. Grow in well-drained, moderately fertile neutral or slightly acid or alkaline soil in full sun to light, dappled shade.

I was often told when running the nursery, 'I've had my bearded Iris for a long time and it has never flowered'. They can take a while to settle in, but the main reason they do not flower is that they have been planted at the wrong depth. Always plant with the rhizome level with the soil, and partially exposed (thinly covered in very hot sites). Do not let other plants overshadow them, they dislike being shaded. They also dislike nitrogen.

PROPAGATION

Sow seed in a cold frame in autumn or spring. Divide rhizomes, it is usual to cut the leaves down to one third and the rhizome can also be cut.

I.chrysographes is a rhizomatous beardless Siberian Iris with linear grey-green leaves to 50cm (20") long . In early summer, each unbranched stem bears 2 fragrant, dark red-violet flowers, up to 7cm (3") across, having gold streaks on the falls. Fully hardy. 40-50cm (16-20").

I.chrysographes 'Black Beauty' is a deep purple black, very balck form afar, with the purple tones showing on closer inspection.

I.chrysographes 'Black Knight' has very dark black flowers. A wow plant.

I.'Before The Storm' is a good example of the red-black colouring.

I.'Black Dragon' is a tall-bearded variety bred by Robert Schreiner in the U.S. Its purple-black flowers appear in mid-late season, they are a velvety deep dark blue-black with matching beards.

I.'Black Gamecock' is a Louisiana hybrid which is an intense dark purple. Not fully hardy. Does well near pond margins.

I.'Black Ink' is a tall bearded variety with very dark blue-black flowers and a good scent.

I.'Black Swan' is a translucent, silky purple contrasting with the broad, black velvet falls. 75cm (30").

A delicious dark bearded Iris named **'Black Taffeta'** could become a firm favourite. It is a deep black violet self. 76cm (30").

I.'Black Watch' is a very dark intermediate with the darkest purple flowers and matching beards with a satin texture. 58cm (23").

I.'Dark Vader' produces ruffled flowers with dark blue-violet standards and black falls with violet beards. 28cm (11").

I.'Deep Black' has very dark purple, almost black flowers. Best in poor soil in full sun. 60cm (2ft).

I.'Demon' has dramatic flowers of the deepest velvety purple, appearing almost black. Purple beards are tipped with gold. The blooms are scented and very floriferous. 30cm (12").

I.'Hello Darkness' is rich and velvety with an unsurpassable degree of black.

I.'Kent Pride' is one perhaps for lovers of brown flowers, its reddish brown petals are most unusual. Interesting rather than desirable. There are others of similar hue.

I.'Langport Midnight' is a deep purple-black self. Free flowering and vigorous. 45cm (18").

I.'Langport Wren' is also of interest with its deep magenta self with black veining on the petals and unusual brown beards. 66cm (26").

I.'Little Black Belt' is the darkest blue-black. 30cm (12").

I.'Purple Landscape' is a purple with bi-colour falls with blue beard, it is a dwarf variety. 40cm (16").

I.'Superstition' is a dark brown-purple,with blue-black beards. 90cm (3ft).

I.'Swazi Princess' is an intensely dark indigo blue with a luxuriant velvety sheen. 91cm (36").

The following dark bearded irises also appear from time to time:
I.'Back in Black','Black Flag', 'Black Hills', 'Black Lady', 'Blackfoot'and 'Clotho'.

I.sibirica 'Tropic Night' has gorgeous flowers of dark purple.

I.spuria 'Stars at Night' has velvety brown-black flowers with clear yellow signals.

KENNEDIA

A woody-stemmed climber from warmer climes with distinctive blackish flowers. Frost tender.

CULTIVATION
Under glass, grow in loam-based compost with added sharp sand in bright, filtered light. Water moderately in growth and apply a balanced feed monthly. Water sparingly in winter.

PROPAGATION
Sow seed under glass in spring. Soak for 12 hours before sowing.

K.nigricans, known as the black coral pea is a robust but frost-tender climber producing racemes of velvety darkest purple-black or dark chocolate flowers with the standard petals reflexed and boldly splashed with a yellow blotch. It will thrive in poor sandy soil and tolerate coastal sites. 4-6m (12-20ft). Minimum 5-7°C (41-45°F).

KNIPHOFIA

Extremely intriguing - a black flowered Red-hot poker, and two with bronze leaves.

K.brachystachya bears small scented black flowers from July to August. 40cm (16").

K.'Dorset Sentry' bears good-sized pokers of a clear bright acid yellow which contrast perfectly with the bronze stems from July to October. Easy and a pleasant form. 1m (3ft).

K.'Mount Etna' has flashing orange -red pokers from brownish stems and buds from August to October. 1.2m (4ft).

LATHYRUS

Perfect climbers for summer screening. Scented flowers are excellent for cutting. I found the black ones a little disappointing, especially on opening, but they do darken. Fabulous combined with whites or pale pinks.

CULTIVATION
Prefer a well-manured and prepared site in the previous autumn to planting. Best in full sun in humus-rich soil and the varieties mentioned here need support. Apply a balanced feed every two weeks when in growth. Dead head, if seed pods are allowed to form, plants stop flowering.

PROPAGATION
Easy from seed. Nicking the seed away from the eye might help germination. Soaking definitely does, greatly improving germination. Seed is best sown in a cold frame in autumn. Can be sown direct into the flowering position in spring.

L.'Black Diamond' bears darkish purple flowers.
L.'Black Knight' has flowers of a dark purple.
L.'Black Prince' bears dark purple flowers.
L.'Bridget' is a dark velvety violet-blue with real depth of colour.
L.'Midnight' is a different colouring, finest dark maroon. Large, frilly flowers on long stout stems. A very vigorous grower.

LEPTINELLA

The button-like flowerheads of one species are very near black. Suitable for paving crevices and gravel gardens. These members of the daisy family are a common feature of the New Zealand alpine flora. Fully hardy.

CULTIVATION
Grow in moderately fertile, sharply drained soil in full sun.

PROPAGATION
Sow fresh seed in containers in an open frame. Divide in spring.

L.atrata (synonym Cotula) is a creeping, tufted perennial with fern-like foliage of a grey-green which can be purple-tinged. In late spring and early summer, it bears purplish-black flowers to 1.5cm across, with yellow anthers becoming prominent as the flower matures. Suitable for an alpine house or scree bed. 15cm (6").

L.atrata ssp luteola differs in having dark red-brown centres and creamy white stigmas. Leaves are less deeply divided.

LEPTOSPERMUM

Attractive plants in leaf and flower with something to offer of interest for those attracted to dark plants. Borderline hardy to frost tender.

CULTIVATION

Under glass, grow in loam-based potting compost in full light, or filtered light. Water freely and apply a balanced feed every month when in growth. Needs little water in winter. May need restrictive pruning. Outdoors, grow in moderately fertile, well-drained soil in full sun or partial shade. They are not tolerant of chalk soils.

PROPAGATION

Sow seed under glass in autumn or spring. Root semi-ripe cuttings with bottom heat in summer.

L.macrocarpum 'Copper Sheen' has deep bronze purplish-green glossy leaves and single reddish flowers. The leaves of the species are also purplish-green. It has unusual flowers where the central, greenish-yellow receptacle is 18mm across, glistening with nectar. The petals are white, marked purple.

The new foliage of **L.petersonii** is bronze-red. The narrow leaves have a lemon-scent when crushed.

L.rupestre turns bronze-purple in very cold weather.

L.scoparium is fairly tender, thriving only in south-western counties of England, in sheltered gardens or against a wall.

L.scoparium 'Black Robin' is a compact shrub of conicle habit bearing dark reddish-purple foliage with numerous flowers of 1cm across, pink with a deep purple almost black centre. Up to 2m (6ft).

L.scoparium 'Burgundy Queen' has bronzed foliage with double red flowers.

L.scoparium 'Chapmannii' bears bronze-coloured foliage, whilst **L.scoparium 'Nanum'** has dark bronzy-green leaves.

The small leaves of **L.scoparium 'Nicholsii'** and of **'Nichollsii Nanum'** are deep bronzy-purple when grown on open ground. **L.scoparium 'Ruby Glow'** is a double-flowered form with bronzy foliage and red stems.

LIGULARIA

These will provide excellent dark foliage and contrasting flowers for moist soil. Imposing by the side of a pond. Fully hardy.

CULTIVATION

Moderately fertile, deep moist soil in full sun. Shelter from strong winds.

PROPAGATION

Divide in spring after flowering. L.dentata 'Desdemona' and L.dentata 'Othello' come relatively true from seed sown outdoors in autumn or spring.

L.dentata 'Dark Beauty' has kidney-shaped leaves which are darkish above and darkish-red beneath. The yellow flowers are smallish and star-shaped. Grows to around 1m (Bill McHugh)

L.dentata 'Desdemona' is a dramatic foliage plant. Huge, heart-shaped glowing bronze- purple leaves are beetroot red beneath, providing a striking contrast to the sprays of orange-yellow daisy flowers held on very dark stems in late summer. 120cm (4ft).

If you can still find it **L.'Moorblut'** has even darker leaves.

L.dentata 'Othello' has puckered bronzy-green leaves with magenta undersides with vivid orange flowers. 120cm (4ft).

Many have dark stems such as the purple stems of **L.dentata 'Sommergold'** and the almost black stems of **'The Rocket'**.

LILIUM

Black lilies, yes as long as you do not expect them to be too dark, they are much darker than the usual reds. You could have a succession of flowers if you grew all three from early to late summer. Fully hardy to frost tender.

CULTIVATION
Prefer well-drained soil enriched with leaf mould, or any well-rotted organic matter. Position in full sun, they dislike shade. Plant bulbs in autumn at a depth of 2-3 times their height.

PROPAGATION
Remove scales, offsets or bulblets from dormant bulbs as the foliage dies down. Remove stem bulbils in late summer.

L.'Black Beauty' is probably the darkest of the three. A vigorous oriental hybrid with turkscap flowers. In midsummer racemes of scented, medium-sized turkscaps of a dark-blackish red are produced with green centres and white tepal margins.1.5m (5ft).
L.'Black Dragon' bears stout racemes of large, scented, outward-facing trumpet-shaped flowers of a dark purplish-red on the outside and white within in early summer. 1.5m (5ft).
L.'Black Magic Group' is a vigorous trumpet-shaped lily flowering in mid-late summer. From maroon buds opening to reddish black on the outside to white within, as the trumpet opens the white predominates, fragrant.1.5m (5ft). The colouring on L.formosanum is similar.
L.nepalense might also be of interest with its large reddish purple blotch inside the yellow to greenish flowers. A rhizomatous lily requiring acid soil and partial shade. Frost tender. Either unscented or unpleasant smelling.

LOBELIA

The hardy perennial lobelias offer some dark foliage plants with red flowers. They are all well worth growing, though you may eventually choose a favourite. Fully hardy.

CULTIVATION
Grow in deep, fertile, reliably moist soil in full sun or partial shade.

PROPAGATION
Sow fresh seed of perennials as soon as ripe, or sow in spring.

L.'Bees'Flame' is a slightly hairy perennial with reddish-purple stems and linear lance-shaped leaves of the same colour. In mid to late summer racemes to 15cm (6") long are borne of brilliant crimson flowers. 75cm (30").
L.'Dark Crusader' bears maroon stems and velvety deep red flowers. 60-90cm (24-36").
L.'Queen Victoria' is a short-lived perennial with deep red-purple stems and lance-shaped leaves of the same colour. From late summer to mid-autumn, the scarlet flowers are borne on racemes to 45cm (18") long. Flowers are slightly smaller than L.'Bees' Flame'. 90cm (3ft).
L.'Queen Victoria' will benefit from a mulch and overwinters better in moist soil. Also worth considering is **L.tupa** because it is simply beautiful with its red-purple stems and its brick-red to brown-red flowers with red-purple calyces borne in racemes to 34cm (18") long. Leaves are grey-green. 2m (6ft). Not fully hardy, but a magnificent plant for a sheltered spot. Can be raised from seed.
L.'Will Scarlet' has bright blood-red flowers over green foliage flushed maroon. 90cm (36").
L.splendens and L.x speciosa cultivars can also bear reddish foliage.

LOPHOSTEMON

Closely related to Myrtus, these evergreen shrubs or small trees can provide us with wonderful dark foliage combined with attractive flowers and berries. Frost hardy to frost tender.

CULTIVATION

Under glass, grow in loam-based compost in bright, filtered light. When in growth, water freely and apply a balanced feed monthly. Requires little water in winter. May need restrictive pruning. Outdoors, grow in fertile, humus-rich, moist but well-drained soil in partial shade.

PROPAGATION

Sow fresh seed under glass. Root semi-ripe cuttings with heels in summer with bottom heat.

L.bullata is a large shrub or small tree with downy stems. Leaves are strongly puckered and bronze or red tinted when young. White flowers, deep black-red berries. 3-8m (10-25ft).

L.bullata 'Matai Bay' differs from the species in that the new shoots are bright red maturing to mahogany brown.

The **x ralphii** cultivars produce some interestingly coloured foliage. **'Indian Chief'** has rounded, lustrous reddish-green foliage, whereas **'Kathryn'** has blistered leaves flushed a rich deep purple. **'Purpurea'** has slightly blistered bronze to red-purple leaves and **'Red Dragon'** has new shoots which are a brilliant reddish pink maturing to an outstanding blackish red, much darker than the foliage on the others, whilst **'Wild Cherry'** bears rich purple-red foliage which intensifies in winter. 1.5-2.5m (5-8ft).

'Lilliput' and **'Pixie'** are two dwarf forms with reddish foliage.

LOROPETALUM

Evergreen shrubs or small trees found in the Himalaya, best grown in woodland. Borderline frost hardy.

CULTIVATION

Grow in fertile, humus-rich, moist but well-drained neutral to acid soil in partial shade. Undemanding but will respond to regular watering and fertiliser. Needs a minimum temperature of 5°C (41°F) to flower well.

PROPAGATION

Sow fresh seed in an open frame. Root semi-ripe cuttings with bottom heat.

L.chinense 'Fire Dance' is a neat, compact evergreen shrub with tiered branches and fuchsia pink flowers in early spring. Purplish red foliage right through the season. Can be grown in a pot. To 2m (6ft).

LYCHNIS

Worthy of being included in the dark border is **L.x arkwrightii 'Vesuvius'.**
A short-lived perennial with very dark, brownish to dark purple foliage and knock-out orange-scarlet flowers in early to midsummer. Fully hardy. 45cm (18").
L.sieboldii has similar colouring. 30cm.

LYSIMACHIA

Offering two forms one with dark foliage and the other with dark flowers which are excellent for the border.
L.atropurpurea available from seed has dark spikes of very dark purple flowers from spring through to summer set off by fleshy glaucous green leaves.
L.ciliata 'Firecracker' is a real cracker with its handsome purple foliage and yellow flowers in midsummer.

MAGNOLIA

Irresistible flowers of astonishing beauty, but not very dark, rich-purple is about the darkest.

CULTIVATION
Grow in moist, well-drained, humus-rich acid to neutral soil in sun or partial shade. Shelter from strong winds. Early-flowering varieties can be damaged by late frosts.

PROPAGATION
Sow seed in autumn in a seedbed. Stratified seed germinates freely, but remember most Magnolias will take many years to flower from seed. Graft in winter. Bud in summer. Layer in early spring.

M.grandiflora 'Gallisoniere' bears leaves of reddish-brown on the underside.
M.liliiflora 'Nigra' is generally acknowledged as being the darkest Magnolia, of great beauty, it is dark in comparison with the purplish pinks of other Magnolias. A compact deciduous shrub, flowering when young and bearing very dark-purple-red flowers of goblet-shape in early summer and intermittently into autumn. Suitable for a small garden. Grow against a wall in colder areas. .2.5m (8ft).
M.liliiflora 'O Neill', at present available in the U.S. has black-purple flowers, the buds being almost black and opening to very dark purple. 4m (12ft).
Watch out for recent developments in New Zealand, where a darker still form is in the pipeline.
M.'Randy' is a cross between M.liliiflora and M.stellata and produces small, darkish purple upright flowers.
M x soulageana 'Amabilis' is a pure white, with a chocolate centre.
M.x soulageana 'Brozzonii' is white on the outside with a purple flush at the base, and is one of the darker cultivars of this species.

MAHONIA

Grown for their handsome foliage, fragrant flowers and berries, these purple-leaved forms should make a good addition to the border. They are fully hardy.

CULTIVATION
Grow in moderately fertile, humus-rich, moist but well-drained soil. Mostly prefer full or partial shade. If in sun, make sure the soil is kept moist.

PROPAGATION
Sow seed outdoors in containers or in a seedbed in autumn or when ripe. Stratified seed germinates freely. Root semi-ripe or leafbud cuttings from late summer to autumn.

M.aquifolium bears foliage which turns purplish in winter.
M.aquifolium 'Atropurpurea' has foliage turning a dark red-purple in winter. Provides a good contrast to the dense clusters of yellow flowers. The leaves of the species itself can also provide similar colouring, though not as dark, in winter. The species and its cultivars offer blue-black berries.1m (3ft).
M.aquifolium develops red tints in the second year, the best colouring is obtained on plants in sun.
M.gracilis bears white flowers which open from purplish buds.
The rich, dark green foliage of **M.nervosa** often turns deep burgundy with the onset of colder weather in winter.
M.x wagneri 'Pinnacle' is upright and has bronze, juvenile leaves, maturing to green. Please note several different hybrids are sold under this name.
M.x wagneri 'Undulata' has dark glossy green foliage with wavy-margined leaflets which turn red-purple in winter. 2m(6ft).

Anthriscus sylvestris 'Ravenswing'

Artemisia lactiflora Guizhou Group

Aquilegia vulgaris 'William Guiness'

Basil 'Spice Boys'

Arisaema griffithii

Begonia rex cultivar

Billardiera longiflora

Canna, purple leaved

Bromeliad

Clematis 'Black Prince'

Chrysanthemum 'Black Magic'

Clematis recta 'Purpurea'

Clematis 'Romantika'

Crinum purpureum

Clematis 'Viola'

Cryptotaenia japonica

Colocasia esculenta

Dahlia coccinea

Dianthus barbatus 'Sooty'

Penstemon digitalis 'Husker Red'

Dianthus Black and White Minstrels Group

Dierama - dark flowered

Dracunculus vulgaris

Eupatorium rugosum 'Chocolate'

Euphorbia amygdaloides 'Purpurea'

Euphorbia dulcis 'Chameleon'

Fritillaria persica 'Adiyaman'

Geranium sinense

Geranium phaeum 'Samobor'
flower detail

Geranium phaeum 'Samobor'
foliage detail

Geranium pratense 'Purple Haze'
foliage detail

Haloragis erecta 'Wellington Bronze'

Geranium pratense 'Purple Haze'
flower detail

Helleborus orientalis hybrids

Helleborus orientalis hybrids

Heuchera micrantha v diversifolia 'Palace Purple'

Helleborus orientalis hybrids

Heuchera 'Velvet Night'

Hemerocallis 'Purple Rain'

Alcea rosea 'Black Beauty'

Hydrangea dark foliage

Iris 'Little Black Belt'

Iris chrysographes

Iris 'Purple Landscape'

Iris 'Demon'

Iris 'Superstition'

Kale 'Red Bor'

Leycesteria formosa

Lathyrus odoratus black

Lysimachia ciliata 'Firecracker'

Lettuce 'Seville'

Lysimachia atropurpurea

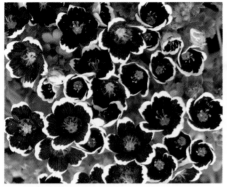

Nemophila 'Pennie Black'

Paeonia delavayi

Nicandra physalodes black pods

Paeonia 'Guan Shi Mo Yu'

Oxalis triangularis

Paeonia 'Hei Hue Kui'

Paeonia 'Hei hue Kui'
different flower form

Perilla frutescens v purpurascens

Paeonia 'Yan Long Zi Zhu Pan'

Pittosporum tenuifolium
'Tom Thumb'

Papaver somniferum 'Chedglow'

Plantago major 'Rubrifolia'

Podophyllum hexandrum

Primula Gold-Laced Group
(polyanthus)

Polemonium yezoense 'Purple Rain'

Purple-leaved shrubs make
eye-catching subjects for hedges

Primula auricula 'Gizabroon'

Ranunculus ficaria 'Brazen Hussy'

Rudbeckia occidentalis
'Green Wizard'

Sempervivum 'Gravpurpur'

Scabiosa 'Chile Black'

Sempervivum 'Jungle Fires'

Sempervivum 'Dark Beauty'

Sempervivum 'Quintessence'

Sempervivum 'Red Devil'

Trillium erectum

Sempervivum 'Rotkopf'

Viola 'Bowles Black'

Torenia fournieri

Viola walteri

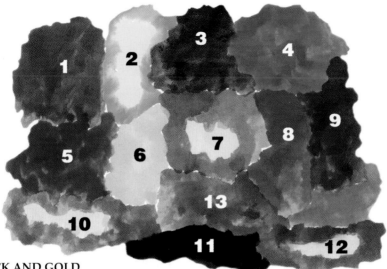

BLACK AND GOLD

1. Berberis thunbergii 'Atropurpurea'
2. Cornus alba 'Spaethii' or Elaeagnus pungens 'Maculata'
3. Sambucus nigra 'Black Beauty'
4. Cotinus coggygria 'Royal Purple'
5. Euphorbia dulcis 'Chameleon'
6. Tulipa and Iris golden yellow or black

7. Rosa 'Happy Child'
8. Lobelia 'Bees' Flame'
9. Tulipa 'Queen of Night'
10. Ranunculus ficaria 'Brazen Hussy'
11. Ophiopogon planiscapus 'Nigrescens'
12. Ranunculus ficaria 'Aglow in the Dark'
13. Heuchera 'Rachel'

BLACK AND SILVER

1. Berberis thunbergii 'Helmond Pillar'
2. Cosmos atrosanguineus
3. Geranium phaeum 'Samobor'
4. Artemisia ludoviciana ssp mexicana v albula
5. Papaver orientale 'Black and White'
6. Heuchera 'Chocolate Ruffles'

7. Antirrhinum majus 'Black Prince'
8. Papaver somniferum Black double
9. Senecio cineraria 'Cirrhus'
10. Ophiopogon planiscapus 'Nigrescens'
11. Celmisia semicordata
12. Viola 'Roscastle Black'
13. Helleborus orientalis black

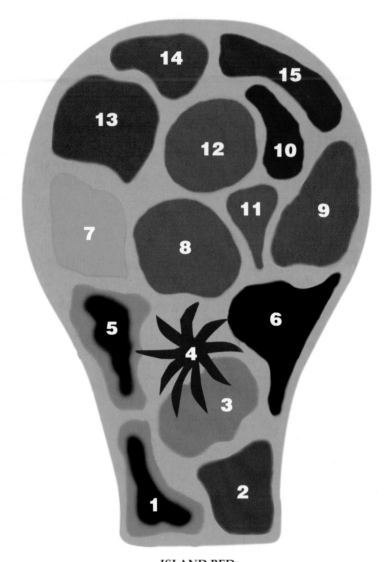

ISLAND BED

1. Erica cinerea 'Velvet Night'
2. Ajuga reptans 'Burgundy Glow'
3. Artemisia absinthium 'Lambrook Silver'
4. Phormium 'Platt's Black'
5. Dianthus Black and White Minstrels Group
6. Ophiopogon planiscapus 'Nigrescens'
7. Stachys byzantina
8. Berberis thunbergii 'Atropurpurea'

9. Heuchera 'Black Velvet'
10. Senecio cineraria 'Silver Dust'
11. Paeonia 'Black Pirate'
12. Acer palmatum 'Atropurpureum'
13. Salvia officinalis Purpurascens Group
14. Haloragis 'Wellington Bronze'
15. Viola 'Bowles' Black'

MALUS

Dark foliage contrasting with pink flowers is on offer from these fully hardy, deciduous trees.

CULTIVATION
Moderately fertile, moist but well-drained soil in full sun for purple-leaved forms.

PROPAGATION
Sow seed in a seedbed in autumn. Bud in late summer or graft in midwinter.

M.x purpurea is an erect, open tree with usually broadly ovate, dark green leaves. The young wood and spring foliage are both purplish red. In mid-spring purplish-red flowers open from ruby red buds and are followed by dark red fruit. Some of its cultivars, often confused with the species, have the same colouring in the foliage, such as **M.'Aldenhamensis', M.'Eleyi' and M.'Lemoinii'**. 4-7m (12-22ft).
M.'Profusion' has bronzy purple leaves, purple-red when young, dark reddish flowers and dark purple fruits.
M.'Red Barron' is a broadly upright tree with ovate bronze-green leaves which are purple when young and contrast well with the dark pink flowers which open from dark buds in late spring and are followed by glossy, dark red fruit. 6m (20ft).
M.'Royalty' is a spreading tree with ovate dark red-purple foliage which retains its colour well and turns red in autumn. Crimson-purple flowers are borne in mid to late spring, followed by dark red fruit. 8m (25ft).
M.tschonoskii is an erect tree with broadly ovate glossy mid-green leaves which provide brilliant autumn colours of orange, red and purple. Pink-flushed white flowers are borne in spring, followed by red-flushed, yellowish fruit. 12m (40ft). The foliage of **M.'Winter Gold'** is bronze-

tinged when young, and that of M.'Wisley' is bronze-red at first, turning green. Other cultivars with dark foliage, usually when young are available.

MARANTA

Cultivated for their handsome leaves with black markings, Marantas are from rainforests in tropical America. They are grown as houseplants in frost-prone areas being frost tender.

CULTIVATION
Under glass, grow in loam-based or loamless compost in bright filtered or bright indirect light. They have shallow root systems and can be grown in half pots. Require high humidity. When in growth, water moderately and apply a balanced feed monthly. Water sparingly in winter. Outdoors, grow in humus-rich, moist but well-drained soil in deep or partial shade.

PROPAGATION
Sow seed when fresh. Divide in spring. Take basal cuttings 7-10cm (3-4") long and root with bottom heat in spring.

M.leuconeura v erythroneura known as the Herringbone plant bears velvety olive and black-green leaves with interesting red midribs and veins. To add to the effect there are jagged light yellow-green markings around the midribs and the undersides are deep red. 30cm (12"). Minimum temperature 15°C (59°F).
M.leuconeura v kerchoveana is more common having black or dark brown squarish markings on the leaves which have led to the common name of rabbit's tracks. Very effective.
M.leuconeura v massangeana has blackish-green foliage with silver-grey feathering along the midribs and veins with purple on the undersides.

MELICA

Grasses provide excellent contrast in the border and are useful for drying. Fully hardy.

CULTIVATION
Grow in moderately fertile, moist but well-drained soil in full sun.

PROPAGATION
Sow fresh seed where you want the plants to grow. Divide as growth starts.

M.altissima 'Atropurpurea' is an attractive ornamental grass bearing erect spikelets with densely flowered tips of a lustrous deep purple, paler as they age in summer. Up to 120cm (4ft).
M.uniflora 'Variegata' has fresh green leaves, marked white and flushed purple at the bases, bearing spikelets of dark purplish-brown flowers in late summer.
M.ciliata bronze and **M.transsilvanica 'Atropurpurea'** will be of interest too.

MISCANTHUS

Make excellent free-standing specimen plants with their showy arching panicles of flowers above reed-like grass. M.sinensis is fully hardy.

CULTIVATION
Tolerant of most conditions. Dislikes excessive winter wet.
PROPAGATION
Sow seed in a cold frame in early spring. Divide in spring. Can be slow to establish.

M.sinensis v purpurascens has foliage which turns purple-green with pink midribs, developing autumn tones. Spikelets of purplish flowers in autumn.
M.sinensis 'Morning Light' bears dark crimson plumes fading to tan. 1.3m.

M.sinensis 'Ferne Osten' has narrowish leaves with wonderful autumn colours of bright copper with dark red tints on leaves. 1.5m
M.sinensis 'Malepartus' makes imposing arches of broad leaves with a central silver vein to contrast with the mahogany red fresh plumes which age to pinkish-buff. 2m (6ft).

MOLINIA

Excellent autumn foliage is provided by the two species of this perennial grass, with graceful panicles of flowers. Fully hardy.

CULTIVATION
Any moist, but well-drained soil. Prefer acid to neutral soil in full sun or partial shade.

PROPAGATION
Seed of species can be sown in a coldframe in spring. Divide in spring and pot up until well-established.

M.caerulea, the purple moor grass, has mid-green leaves to 45cm (18") long with purple bases. From summer to autumn it bears narrow panicles of purple spikelets on contrasting yellow-tinted stems. 1.5m (5ft).
Some of the cultivars also have dark flowers, such as **M.caerulea ssp arundinacea 'Karl Foerster'** which has leaves to 80cm (32") long and bears spikelets of purple flowers on arching stems.
M.caerulea ssp arundinacea 'Moorhexe' is perhaps the darkest with its panicles of dark purple spikelets held tightly against erect stems.
M.caerulea ssp caerulea 'Edith Dudszus' is a shorter variety with green leaves and almost erect black flower heads. 42cm (15").

NAUTILOCALYX

Evergreen, perennial gesneriads from tropical America make excellent greenhouse plants. Frost tender.

CULTIVATION
Under glass, grow in loamless potting compost in bright filtered light. Water freely during growth and apply a balanced feed monthly. Reduce watering in winter. Require high humidity and a minimum temperature of 16°C (61°F).

PROPAGATION
Root softwood or stem tip cuttings in spring or summer.

N.bullatus (synonym N.tesselatus) bears green leaves with a bronze sheen above, purple undersides.
N.lynchii is an erect-branched perennial with delightful toothed glossy green leaves to 12cm (5") which are sometimes red-purple on the surface, being that colour on the underside. Attractive flowers are borne from spring to summer.
N.pemphidius is a very attractive plant with puckered chocolate brown leaves forming a low rosette. Bears small, appealing white flowers.

NEMATANTHUS

I am not convinced of the blackness of the leaves of this Gesneriad, but I am told by Dibley's that **N.'Black Magic'** bears near black glossy leaves and wonderfully contrasting orange flowers. It is very attractive. Grow in soil suitable for African Violets and leave slightly pot-bound for the best flowers. Tropical plant requiring indirect light and high humidity. Not too difficult to grow. Minimum temperature required is 10-15°C.

NEMOPHILA

An easy to grow annual with delightful near black flowers. Fully hardy.

CULTIVATION
Fertile, moist but well-drained soil in full sun or partial shade. Water well to maintain flowering in hot weather.

PROPAGATION
Sow seed outdoors in early spring or autumn where they are to flower. Self-seeds freely. Sold under various names in seed catalogues.

N.'Pennie Black' is a little gem and useful for filling in gaps. Bears pinnate green leaves and produces saucer-shaped flowers of a very dark purple, near black.15-30cm (6-12").

NEOREGELIA

More bromeliads producing green leaves which are purplish towards the base. Grow as for other bromeliads.

N.concentrica has yellow-white bracts in the centre, turning purple-pink in summer. **N.concentrica v plutonis** is similar having the extra allurement of its leaves being flushed dark magenta-red.
N.concentrica 'Aztec' bears green leaves all marked heavily with purplish-brown.
N.eleutheropetala has mid-green leaves, turning reddish-green towards the base. The innermost purple-brown leaves surround dense umbel-like inflorescences of white flowers, intriguingly and attractively interspersed with long, purple-tipped bracts. Others of interest are **N.chlorostica, N.marmorata and N.spectabilis and the Claret Group.** Minimum temperature 10°C.

NEPENTHES

Curioser and curioser, the pitchers of these carnivorous plants are often marked with purple or red. Interesting rather than beautiful.Pitchers secrete nectar to attract insects and small mammals which become trapped inside.Frost tender.

CULTIVATION
All species need a warm greenhouse if grown where temperatures generally fall below 10°C at night, higher for some species, see below. Requiring high humidity and ventilation in very high temperatures.

PROPAGATION
Sow fresh seed on the surface of moist coir compost and place in a tray of water in a shaded propagator at a constant temperature of 27°C (81°F). Cuttings with 3-4 leaves can be inserted into coir compost maintaining the same temperature or a little lower than above. Air layer in spring or summer.

N.ampullaria has pitchers of a deep red or green, sometimes mottled.
N.x coccinea bears pitchers up to 15cm (6") long, mottled purple-red.
N.'Director G.T.Moore' has dense purple-red mottling on its pitchers.
The upper pitchers of **N.gracilis** are often mahogany-red.
N.mirabilis has pitchers spotted red.
The curious creamy-green pitchers of **N.rafflesiana** are attractively marked chocolate-red, each with a striped rim. Minimum temperature 24°C daytime, 15°C nighttime, 21°C in winter.
N.rajah has pitchers to 35cm (14") long which are mottled red to red-purple.

NYMPHAEA

Water lilies are a decorative addition to any pool. The shade of their leaves reduces algae and their flowers are unbelievably beautiful. Fully to frost hardy.

CULTIVATION
Grow in undisturbed water in full sun. Plant in firm, loamy soil inserting the rhizomes just under the surface and covering with washed pea gravel. Submerge.

PROPAGATION
Surface sow fresh seed and cover with 2.5cm (1") of water, hardy species need a germinating temperature of 10-13°C. The seed heads of water lilies sink as the seed ripens. Divide rhizomes or separate offsets.

N.'Atropurpurea' has semi-double dark red flowers, the young foliage is purple turning to dark green.
N.'Black Opal' is an intensely deep red, overlaid with a sheen of black.
N.'Black Princess' is a deep red, blackish towards the centre on large flowers.
N.'Perry's Darkest Red' is a very similar colouring to the above.
N.'William Falconer' the darkest red before the arrival of the new lilies bred in America. Leaves splashed with brown.
A number of Nymphaea also bear foliage which is red, often only when young, or marked or flecked red, these include N.'Caroliniana', N.'James Brydon', N.'Laydeckeri Fulgens', N.'Laydeckeri Lilacea', N.'Laydeckeri Purpurata', N.'Madame Maurice Laydecker', N.'Perry's Red Star', N.'Pygmaea Rubis' , N'Sirius', N.'Pearl of the Pool' whose leaves are bronze when young and N.'Lucida' having leaves heavily marked with purple.

OPHIOPOGON

This plant, the so-called Black Grass, even though it is not a grass, is the one that started off my interest in black plants many years ago. Resist it if you can. Fully hardy.

CULTIVATION
Grow in moist but well-drained slightly acid, fertile, humus-rich soil in full sun. Give a dressing of leaf mould every autumn.

PROPAGATION
Can be sown from seed, but only expect a percentage to come true and watch for green at the bases which really spoils the effect. Sow fresh seed in a cold frame. Divide in spring as growth resumes.

O.planiscapus 'Nigrescens' goes under many synonyms but they should all be named as above, you may find it listed as 'Arabicus', 'Black Knight' or 'Black Dragon' or 'Ebony Knight'. Has the blackest leaves of any plant. It is a clump-forming, slowly spreading, rhizomatous perennial. Its arching, strap-shaped, spidery leaves make an all year round feature. In summer, it bears short sprays of tiny mauvish bells, and the shiny black berries last well into winter. 20cm (8").
The Japanese use it as a grass substitute and it is excellent for edging or could be used to good effect in a rock garden. Associates well with pink flowers or silvery foliage and looks magnificent with snowdrops scattered around and through its leaves.
Truly remarkable for its colour, can look silvery in full sun. My number one black plant, if you only want to grow one black foliage plant, then this is the one to choose. Easy to grow, and trouble free.

ORBEA

Sometimes placed under Stapelia to which it is closely related. Flowers are therefore, often unpleasantly scented. Frost tender.

CULTIVATION
Under glass, grow in standard cactus compost, top dress with grit. Provide bright filtered light in summer, with low humidity and full light in winter. From spring to early autumn water freely, applying a low-nitrogen fertiliser monthly. At other times of the year, keep dry, watering sparingly if it is warm in winter to prevent shrivelling. Outdoors, grow in gritty, loamy, moderately fertile, humus-rich soil in partial shade.

PROPAGATION
Sow seed under glass in spring. Take stem-segments in spring and summer.

O.variegata is a variable, clump-forming succulent. It bears extraordinary flowers of a unique beauty in summer. Funnel-shaped, flat, densely wrinkled dark brownish-red flowers 5-9cm (2-3.5") across are marked with white, or creamy-yellow. Stems can also be purplish. 10cm (4").

ORBEOPSIS

This genus may sometimes be found under Caralluma. Grow as above. Frost tender.

O.albocastanea has reddish brown stems. In early summer, star-shaped flowers are borne. Green on the outside, marked with red spots and cream on the inside marked with brownish-purple spots, with a deep brown corona.

ORTHOPHYTUM

Bromeliads which spread by stolons to form rosettes of usually stemless, softly spiny leaves, some with colours other than just green. Frost tender.

CULTIVATION
Under glass, grow in a compost suitable for terrestrial bromeliads in full light. Water moderately with soft water in the growing season. Apply a half-strength, balanced feed once a month. In winter, keep plants dry. Outdoors, grow in sharply drained, moderately fertile, humus-rich soil in full sun. Minimum temperature 15°C (59°F).

PROPAGATION
Sow seed in early spring under glass. Separate offsets in spring.

O.gurkenii is a curious bromeliad with purple-brown leaves strikingly barred with silvery lines. Bears brilliant green flowers with bracts similar to the leaves.
O.navioides often turns bright red or red-purple as the flowers mature, being green prior to that. Bears white flowers. 20cm (8").

O.vagans is a trailing bromeliad with an elongated, branching caudex, the branches rooting down and forming large, spreading groups. The bright green leaves turn red-purple with age. Stemless inflorescences of apple-green flowers with red or orange bracts are produced in summer. 20cm (8".)

OXALIS

The great, late Geoff Hamilton, once dismissed all Oxalis as weeds, but I cannot agree. The deep purple leaves of those below make them well-worth growing. Fully hardy to frost tender.

CULTIVATION
Plant the tiny rhizomes just below the surface of the soil. Requires well-drained, fertile, humus-rich soil. Water moderately in growth and apply a balanced feed every month. Keep barely moist in winter when dormant.

PROPAGATION
Divide in spring. Small sections of rhizome root readily with bottom heat. I have sometimes divided a pot in spring, next spring it is brimful once more.

O.triangularis 'Cupido' has very dark purple leaves and soft pink flowers. A seed company is selling this as 'Ace of Spades'. **O.triangualris ssp papilionacea 'Atropurpurea'** has the same dark purple leaf with an attractive lighter purple-maroon splash and the flowers a deeper shade of rose-pink. **O.rubra** is similar.
Kevin of Beeches Nursery tells me that these have become muddled over time. The plant I grow has the leaves of the second described here, but with a soft lilac flower. Whichever you grow it is the leaves that matter in this plant and they are a wonderful purple. They fold into what look like butterflies (papilionacea) and are fascinating. I keep mine in a pot outdoors, I have tried it in the garden, but it disappears and it is well-suited to a pot looking truly magnificent right through summer . As the weather turns cooler, I put it into the cold frame, keeping it on the dry side and it comes back year after year. Can be prone to rust.

PAEONIA

Large, showy flowers of an impeccable beauty. Like most extraordinarily beautiful flowers, they do not flower for long, blooms are fairly fleeting. Fully to frost hardy.

CULTIVATION
Grow in deep, fertile, humus-rich soil. Prefer moist but well-drained soil in full sun or partial shade. Shelter from wind.

PROPAGATION
Sow seed in containers outdoors in autumn or early winter. Divide herbaceous peonies in autumn or early spring. Take root cuttings in winter. Take semi-ripe cuttings of peonies in summer or graft in winter.

P.'Black Pirate' is a dramatic deep mahogany red, very dark towards the centre, with black flares. Semi-double flowers open at an angle resembling small trumpets. The foliage is finely cut on this vigorous but compact plant. Saunders American hybrid tree-peony. 1m (3ft).

P.'Chinese Dragon' does not look as dark to me, but is described by Kelways as having semi-double, purplish red flowers with black flares. The irridescent petals appear blue as they reflect the light. Another Saunders introduction. 1m (3ft).

P.'Chocolate Soldier' is an herbaceous perennial with deep green leaves, flushed bronze when young. Bears large, satiny, deeply cupped, semi-double, deep purple -red to chocolate flowers. 1m (3ft).

The species, **P.delavayi** is also quite dark, often raised from seed the flowers are small 8cm (3") across and vary in colour from blood red to deep maroon and almost chocolate brown. Forms a large shrub up to 150cm (5ft).

P.'Guan Shi Mo Yu' is a black-purple with a sheen, bearing large upright flowers with large leaves tinged purple. Described to me by Shuo Wang as the best 'black' one.

P.'Hei Sa Jin' is mulberry with a sheen, lotus shape flowers.

P.'Hui Hua Kui' is also mulberry with a sheen, of chrysanthmum shape with purplish leaves and stalks.

P.'Mai Fleri' has dark, bronzy foliage.

P.'Qing Long Wo Mo Chin' bears long pointed greenish-yellow buds opening to black-purple flowers with conspicuous green pistils. Leaves yellowish green.

P.'Santorb' is a jewel among reds, an intensely rich, dark crimson maroon introduced by Kelways in 1925. It has good stiff stems and is sweetly scented. Late flowering, into July. 66cm (26").

P.suffruticosa 'Hana-daijin' is a double-flowered peony of the darkest red, again with black undertones. Superb.

P.suffruticosa 'Kokuryu-nishiki' (synonym 'Black Dragon Brocade') has very dark red single flowers with blackish undertones in the centre. An absolutely oustanding colour.

P.suffruticosa 'Rimpo' (synonym 'Bird of Rimpo') not as dark as the above but very deep towards the centre.

Some peonies also have bronze foliage such as **P.'Yachiyo-tsubaki'**.

P.'Yan Long Zi Zhu Pan' bears black-purple flowers. It is erect and free-flowering.

PANICUM

Another grass which offers purple colouring. Attractive and ornamental, giving excellent contrast to other plants. Fully hardy.

CULTIVATION
Moderately fertile, well-drained soil in full sun.

PROPAGATION
Sow seed in spring. Divide perennials between mid-spring and late autumn.

P.miliaceum 'Violaceum' is an erect, clump-forming annual with purple-violet leaves, sometimes flushed purple to 40cm (16") long. Produces intricately branched panicles to 30cm (12") long of slightly pendent purple flowers borne in small spikelets in late summer. 90cm (36").

P.virgatum 'Hanse Herms' has a fountain-like habit and rich reddish-purple autumn foliage. 1m (3ft).

P.virgatum 'Heavy Metal' is an amazing steely grey in sun or part shade. Can reach 1.5m. (4.5ft).

P.virgatum 'Rehbraun' bears foliage which is very reddish. 60cm (2ft).

P.virgatum 'Rotstrahlbusch' is a larger plant turning very red early on. It has also been sold under the above name.

P.virgatum 'Rubrum' has foliage tinted reddish-brown in late summer.

P.virgatum 'Squaw' has green foliage turning reddish purple with red flowers.

PAPAVER

Sumptuous silky petals on large cupped flowers dressed in black. Easy to grow from seed or buy a named cultivar. Decorative seedheads follow the flowers and hold many, many seeds. Shake them and they are like pepperpots. The ones described here are fully hardy.

CULTIVATION
Grow in deep, fertile, well-drained soil in full sun.

PROPAGATION
Best to sow seed in situ as they dislike being transplanted. Beware when shaking seedheads, they hold hundreds of seeds. Divide perennials in spring or take root cuttings in late autumn or winter.

P.orientale 'Black and White' is a clump forming perennial which spreads by runners. It has erect, bristly stems and mid-green leaves to 30cm (12") long with lance-shaped toothed segments. Produces white flowers with a large crimson-black mark at the base of each petal.
I cannot see much difference between the above and the seed sold under the name of P.orientale **'Choir Boy',** which is now circulating as a new cultivar.
P.orientale 'Snow Goose' also looks the same or very similar. 1m (3ft).
P.orientale 'Patty's Plum' if you get a good one, is quite dark.
P.orientale 'Royal Chocolate Distinction' sounds different, a deep brown toned red.

P.somniferum 'Black Paeony' is a double peony-flowered poppy of a delicious shade of dark maroon-purple. Stunning. The P.orientale cultivars are marked with blackish blotches at the base of the petals as is P.bracteatum.

PELARGONIUM

Wonderful plants both species and hybrids, most dark flowers seem to fall in the Regal Pelargonium section. Some zonals offer dark foliage too. Frost tender.

CULTIVATION

Under glass, grow in loam-based or loamless compost in full light with shade from hot sun amd good ventilation. Water moderately during growth, applying a balanced feed every 10-14 days in spring and early summer, followed by a high-potash fertiliser when in flower. Water sparingly in winter. Plants kept at a temperature above 7°C (45°F) will most likely continue to flower through winter. Can be cut back up to two thirds and kept almost dry and frost free.

Outdoors, grow in fertile, neutral to alkaline, well-drained soil. Regal cultivars prefer partial shade and zonals prefer sun, though they are tolerant of a little shade. Re-pot overwintered plants in late winter as new growth resumes. Dead-head regularly.

PROPAGATION

Sow seed under glass in late winter and early spring. Take softwood cuttings in spring or late summer and early autumn.

P.'Ann Hoysted' is a vigorous regal with dark red flowers, the upper petals being almost black.

P.'Barbe Bleu' is a purple-black flowered ivy-leaved pelargonium, fading to wine-red in full sun.

P.'Bewerley Park' is a black zoned leaf with contrasting biscuit-pink flowers.

P.'Black Knight' is a single-flowered miniature zonal pelargonium which would be rather disappointing if you assumed from its name that it is black because it bears salmon flowers.

P.'Black Knight' unfortunately sharing the same name as above, but this time a decorative pelargonium, it has purple-black petals, edged with lavender. Flowers are small.

P.'Black Magic' has the darkest mahogany-black flowers.

P.'Black Pearl' bears flowers with a black blaze overlaid with cerise-red.

P.'Black Prince' is a regal pelargonium bearing purple-black blooms which shade into the throat, with white edging.

P.'Black Velvet' is an old regal variety, with very dark velvet black, large flowers, having a light purple edge around the petals. A strong grower.

P.'Bronze Velvet' is a regal with flowers the colour of its name and darker blotches.

P.'Brown's Butterfly' (synonym 'Black Butterfly') is described as having black flowers flecked with mahogany.

P.'Caligula' is a miniature, double-flowered zonal pelargonium with very dark green, almost black leaves, bearing scarlet flowers. Best indoors.

P.'Dark Mabel' (syn. 'Dark Presidio') is a regal with rose-pink flowers with purple-black on the upper petals.

P.'Dark Secret' is another regal with flowers a deep mahogany feathered burgundy.

P.'Dark Venus' is also a dark mahogany regal.

P.'Etna' is a miniature zonal with scarlet flowers and perfectly contrasting black leaves.

P.'Friesdorf' is a dwarf, fancy-leaved zonal pelargonium with rounded, almost black leaves and narrow-petalled, single crimson flowers.

P.'Gordano Midnight' sounds intriguing with its dark, mahogany, almost black flowers on a short, bushy regal.

P.'Lord Bute' is a purple-black, edged wine regal and long considered one of the darkest. It is an excellent regal for bedding.

P.'Madame Fournier' is a delightful miniature, single-flowered zonal pelargonium with purple-black leaves and stems, bearing scarlet flowers.

P.'Marchioness of Bute' is almost black, edged purple. The petals are well-crimped giving the appearance of a double flower to this regal.

P.'Morwenna' is a dark purple-maroon, shading to black regal.

P.'Pompeii' is nearly black, narrowly edged pinky-white. A short, bushy regal which is very distinctive.

P.'Princess Josephine' is a regal bearing flowers of pinkish-purple with a black blaze and feathering.

P.'Red Black Vesuvius' (syn. 'Black Vesuvius') is a scarlet flowered miniature zonal with black leaves.

P.'Rio Grande' is an ivy-leaved with almost black flowers with a white reverse.

P.'Rogue' is a regal with huge mahogany-crimson flowers shading almost to black.

P.'Springfield Black' is a very deep darkest red-black with large blooms, and is probably one of the darkest regals.

P.'Timothy Clifford' is a zonal miniature with such dark green leaves as to almost appear black. Lovely double, salmon-pink flowers.

P.'Voodoo' is a unique pelargonium with light wine-red flowers , blazed purple-black on each petal. Striking.

Several zonal-leaved pelargoniums display a black zone on their leaves, enhanced by the other leaf colours.

There are also a number of flowers in varying colours, but feathered in black such as **P.'Wookey'** and **P.'Zulu King'**.

Of the ivy-leaved pelargoniums, you would probably find **'Tomcat'** to be one of the darkest reds.

PENNISETUM

Some purplish tones are also found amongst these ornamental grasses. The species below are frost hardy.

CULTIVATION
Preferably light, moderately fertile soil in full sun.

PROPAGATION
Sow seed in early spring. Divide in spring or summer.

P.purpureum (Syn setaceum 'Purpureum' and 'Rubrum'?) has dark purple leaves and from midsummer to early autumn bears plumed, deep crimson flowers. Very attractive and often grown as an annual. 1m (3ft).

P.setaceum'Burgundy Giant' is larger than the species and is deep burgundy-purple throughout. Pendulous panicles of flowers are 30cm (12") long. Grows to 1.5m (5ft).

The frost hardy **P.alopecuroides 'Hameln'** is interesting too, early flowering grey-greenish spikelets of flowers mature to a grey-brown. The dark green leaves turning golden yellow in autumn.

The cultivar **'Moudry'** has purple-black flowerheads, above dark green leaves. There was also a black in circulation a few years ago, but it might possibly have been the same as the above.

PENSTEMON

Offering some dark-leaved forms and flowers, see Also Dark section, Penstemons should find a place in the border. Fully hardy to half-hardy.

CULTIVATION
Border perennials need to be grown in fertile, well-drained soil in full sun or partial shade. In areas prone to frosts, protect with a good dry mulch. Dead-head to maintain vigour.

PROPAGATION
Sow seed in late winter or spring. Take softwood cuttings in early summer or semi-ripe in midsummer. Divide in spring.

P.digitalis 'Husker Red' has beetroot-coloured stems and foliage forming the perfect background to the swaying clusters of green buds which open to palest pastel pink or white tubular flowers in early to midsummer. 90cm (3ft).
P.hirsutus normally has green leaves but there is a bronze form to look out for. Fully hardy spreading subshrub.
P.whippleanus has deep mauve, almost black flowers.

PEPEROMIA

Grown mainly for their attractive leaves of varying hue. Tropical and subtropical plants from various habitats. Try small species in terrariums. Frost tender.

CULTIVATION
Under glass, grow in loam-based or loamless compost in bright indirect light when in growth and in full light when dormant. Water moderately in summer, less in winter, will appreciate tepid soft water and do avoid splashing the leaves which mark easily. From spring to summer require high humidity and need to be misted. Apply a balanced feed monthly. Outdoors, grow in humus-rich, moist but well-drained soil in partial shade. Water is absorbed from the atmosphere and stored in leaf cells, therefore the thicker, fleshy leaved varieties can survive for some time in dry conditions. Minimum temperature 15°C (59°).

PROPAGATION
Collect and sow fresh seed under glass (not easy to obtain commercially). When in active growth, take softwood, leaf or leaf bud cuttings. Remove offsets of rosette-leaf types.

P.caperata 'Luna Red' has dark crimson stems with heart-shaped leaves in the same matching hue, silvered and deeply corrugated and veined. 20cm (8").
P.caperata 'Teresa' has bronze-purple leaves.
P.metallica bears dark red leaves with a silver band down the centre. 20cm (8").
P.obtusifolia 'Columbiana' bears fleshy leaves of a rich purple. 25cm (10").
P.rubella bears pale-veined, pale to dark green leaves being red on the underside, giving a copper effect to the surfaces. 20cm.

PERILLA

Cultivated in Japan as a salad crop and herb, but here mainly used for its decorative purple-leaved foliage which is aromatic. Frost hardy.

CULTIVATION
Grow in fertile, moist but well-drained soil in full sun or partial shade. Insignificant flowers need to be removed to prevent self-seeding. Can be planted out early in the season, will withstand light frosts.

PROPAGATION

Sow seed in spring.

P.frutescens v purpurascens is an attractive foliage plant bearing usually dark purple or dark bronze leaves. 45cm (18").

PERSICARIA

P.microcephala 'Red Dragon' looks set to be a big hit. The species is often invasive, so watch the habit of this clonal selection carefully and keep it containerised. It bears bright, metallic red stems and metallic, pewter foliage. An extremely attractive plant with unusual colouring which will cause comment.

PHORMIUM

Ideal for coastal gardens, but irrestible elsewhere, Phormiums are superb foliage plants, making excellent focal points. Frost hardy to half hardy, may tolerate temperatures as low as -12°C (10°F) if given a deep mulch. Older plants are hardier than young ones and P.tenax is the hardiest species.

CULTIVATION

Grow in fertile, moist, but well-drained soil in full sun. Protect in frost-prone areas with a deep dry mulch before the first frosts and by wrapping the plant.

PROPAGATION

Sow seed in spring. Cultivars will not normally come true, although you can expect purple seedlings from P.tenax purpureum. Divide cultivars in spring.

P.tenax 'Bronze Baby' produces tufts of bold, stiff bronzy wine-red leaves, pendent at the tips. Reddish flowers are occasionally produced on purple stems during summer. 45-60cm (18-24").

P.'Chocolate' is another for the chocolate garden. Quite vigorous, grows to 1.2m.

P.'Dark Delight' has foliage the colour of plain dark chocolate, verging on red-brown. 1-1.2m (3-4ft).

P'Dazzler' has arching bronze leaves, striped mahogany, orange and pink. 1m.

P.'Dusky Challenger' has dark brownish leaves, similar to 'Dark Delight'.

P.'Firebird' is a new variety from Margaret Jones of New Zealand producing gorgeous deep red leaves with bright red edges. Upright habit and as hardy as they come.

P.'Fountains' has pewter-grey evergreen foliage, bearing black and gold flowers in June-July. Sounds wonderful.1m (3ft).

P.'Jack Spratt' is a dwarf species making a compact clump of bronzy brown foliage.

P.'Platt's Black' is one of the darkest with near black, narrow foliage of compact habit, slow growing. According to my American friend, this is the darkest she has seen, although there are green hints in the foliage, but Gary Dunlop tells me it is a green leaf with merely a black edge. Two different plants circulating under the same name perhaps. See before you buy.

P.'Purple Giant' reaches vast proportions in its native New Zealand, less so here.

P.tenax 'Coffee' is an interesting colour quite aptly named, the foliage less upright than most others.

P.tenax 'Nanum Purpureum' this dwarf form has brownish-purple leaves. 40cm.

P.tenax Purpureum Group has rich mahogany-purple to dark copper leaves and prefers an open site. Choose a really dark one. 1m (3ft), but is capable of reaching a gigantic 2.5m (8ft).

P.'Thumbelina' has bronze red leaves and a dwarf habit.

PHYLLOSTACHYS

Dramatic black canes on this slow-growing bamboo. A good container subject. Fully hardy.

CULTIVATION
Grow in fertile, humus-rich, moist soil, well-drained in full sun. In frost prone areas, grow in a position protected from strong, cold winds. Protect emerging shoots from slugs.

PROPAGATION
Divide in spring.

P.nigra, the black bamboo is a clump-forming species with arching, slender canes which turn from green to a lustrous black in their second or third year. Abundant lance-shaped, dark-green leaves 4-13cm (1.5-5") long. Reaches a height of 3-5m (10-15ft).
P.violascens is a clump-forming then spreading bamboo with swollen green canes, green at first finely striped purple, becoming violet. Bears narrowly, lance-shaped, glossy green foliage to 12cm (5") long which is glaucous on the undersides. 5m (16ft) or more.

PHYSOCARPUS

An unusual recent introduction with dark foliage on this deciduous shrub. Fully hardy.

CULTIVATION
Prefers acid soil. Moist but well-drained in full sun or partial shade. May become chloritic if grown in shallow chalk soil.

PROPAGATION
Take greenwood cuttings in summer. Remove rooted suckers in spring or autumn.

P.opulifolius 'Diabolo' has spiny purple to very dark red-black leaves which are useful for flower arranging. I have read one or two descriptions of the leaf colour which are not becoming. It is a plant to see first and decide if the colouring is what you are looking for. I find it agreeable enough. There certainly does not seem to be anything else of quite the same hue. Flowers are produced in summer followed by bladder-like fruit. 1-2m (3-6ft).

PITTOSPORUM

Glossy, leathery leaves in very good colour tones. Good for coastal regions. Excellent specimen plants in warmer areas. Frost hardy to frost tender. Half hardy species may survive temperatures of below 0°C (32°F) for short spells, provided wood has been well ripened in summer.

CULTIVATION
Under glass, grow in loam-based potting compost in full light. In growth, water moderately, applying a balanced fertiliser monthly. Water sparingly in winter. Outdoors, grow in fertile, moist but well-drained soil in full sun for dark-leaved varieties described below. Shelter from wind. Trim hedges in spring.

PROPAGATION
Seed is best sown fresh or in spring in a cold frame. Take semi-ripe cuttings in summer, layer or air layer in spring.

P.tenuifolium 'Atropurpureum' bears purple foliage.
The seed-raised **P.t. 'James Stirling'** has blackish-purple branchlets.
P.tenuifolium 'Nigricans' produces black twigs and deep bronze-purple mature leaves. Excellent for cut foliage.

P.tenuifolium 'Nutty's Leprechaun' is about half the size of 'Tom Thumb'. 50cm (1.5ft). (Gary Dunlop).

P.tenuifolium 'Purpureum' has purple foliage, being similar to 'Nigricans', but more open in habit. 3m (10ft).

P.tenuifolium 'Tom Thumb' forms a low bush with wonderful bronze-purple glossy foliage as it matures, new growth is light green. 1m (3ft).

PLANTAGO

Handsome decorative plantains are available which are not at all invasive.

CULTIVATION
Prefer moist but well-drained soil, do not allow them to dry out. Unfussy.

PROPAGATION
Sow seed of species in autumn in a cold frame. Some cultivars come true, including 'Rubrifolia' listed here. Divide in spring.

P.lanceolata 'Streaker' bears variegated foliage and tubby dark brown flowers. Does not self-seed. Suitable for a pot, will not tolerate acid soil.

P.major 'Rubrifolia' is a good foliage plant which is easy to grow and should not become invasive, although it seeds itself freely, it does not become a nuisance. Bears very large, wide, beetroot coloured foliage which is deeply veined. Spiky brown seedheads are useful for drying. 30cm.

PODOPHYLLUM

Shade-loving plants with bronze foliage and contrasting white cupped flowers. Fully hardy.

CULTIVATION
Grow in humus-rich, moist soil in full, partial or dappled shade. Ideally suited to woodland or a moist, shady border.

PROPAGATION
Sow fresh seed in an open frame.

P.hexandrum bears marbled bronze foliage which emerges and unfolds like an umbrella after flowering. Pure white, sometimes pink, cupped flowers are followed by large, brilliant red fruits. Watch out for slugs. 45cm (18"). TOXIC: all parts if ingested.

POLEMONIUM

Bronzed-foliage on a Jacob's ladder provides interest on these well-known plants. Fully hardy.

CULTIVATION
Grow in any fertile, moist, well-drained soil in full sun or partial shade. Dead-head regularly.

PROPAGATION
Sow seed in a cold frame in autumn or spring. Divide in spring.

P.'Sonia's Bluebell' has dark bronzed foliage with pale blue flowers having white centres.

P.yezoense 'Purple Rain' produces a fine basal rosette of bronzed-purple foliage from which arise stems of purple ladders. Attractive rich lilac flowers are 2.5cm (1") across. Comes true from seed, discard any seedlings not dark enough. 45cm (18").

PRIMULA

Most of the dark-flowered Primulas fall into the Auricula group. Astonishing and amazingly beautiful flowers, little wonder they attracted very high prices in the past. Irresistible plants with sumptuous flowers in colours including brown, black and deepest reds and purples. Fully hardy to frost tender.

CULTIVATION
Generally, P.auricula will grow in full sun with midday shade, or in partial shade. A moist, but gritty, sharply drained soil is required. Prefers humus-rich, slightly alkaline soil. Some alpine species require the protection of an alpine house. Border varieties are not quite so fussy.

PROPAGATION
Surface sow seed in spring. Remove offsets in autumn or early spring.

P.'Barbarella' is a nearly black self whose dark colouring contrasts dramatically with the attractive foliage. A strong-growing plant.
P.'Blackfield' is a self which bears red flowers.
P.'Blackhill' is a self which is a dark red.
P.'Black Ice' bears purple-brown self flowers.
P.'Butterwick' is a sturdy-growing alpine auricula with rich velvety-brown flowers.
P.'Consett' is a dark red self.
P.'Cortina' is a dark red self acclaimed for the velvety texture of its flowers and its thickly mealed foliage.
P.'C.W.Needham' is an alpine auricula that can always be relied upon to produce a wealth of dark purple flowers with almost white centres of an incredible velvety texture. Raised in 1939.
P.'Douglas Black' is another dark red self.

P.'Dusky Maiden' is an alpine auricula with dark purple-brown shades.
P.'Eden Simon' is a fairly dark border auricula of a shade of deep purple with a light centre.
P.'Freda' is a stunning, unrivalled black self. Worth seeking.
P.'Guizabroon' is a dark red self with handsome mealed leaves. Raised by Derek Telford, who has produced many good dark reds. The photograph I have looks very dark, my plant has not flowered yet, so I await in anticipation.
P.'Karen Cordray' is a black and white striped auricula with somewhat variable flowers. Best in a cold greenhouse, although they are hardy.
P.'Matthew Yates' is a purple-black double-flowered auricula.
P.'Merlin' is also a black and white stripe.
P.'Mikado' listed since 1906 has a fine truss of black pips contrasting well with the long green serrated leaves.
P.'The Raven' very dark red-black flowers on this self.
P.'The Snods' is a dark show self, appears almost black, raised in the 1960's and its name taken from a small village in the north of England.
P.'Trouble' if you wish to add to your chocolate selection, this is the one for you, a double-flowered auricula in a shade of light chocolate.
P.'Typhoon' is an alpine auricula bearing brownish-purple flowers with a contrasting gold centre.
P.'Wincha' is a very dark red-black self.

The hardy Barnhaven strain also offer some dark flowers and foliage. Other primroses and polyanthus are listed below. Do not allow these to dry out. Divide regularly.

P.'Bergfruhlung Julianas Group' (PO) includes deep blue shades with a yellow eye and dark green leaves tinged bronze. P.'Cowichans Group' (PO) has some intense blues, some with black centres, and black-garnet shades, you can find these as mixes or as separate colours such as 'Cowichan Garnet Group'. All have reddish brown tinted foliage.
P.'Firefly Group' (PO) bears deep velvety red flowers with bronzed foliage.
P.'Gold-Laced Group' (PO) is a beautiful old-fashioned flower which if you only grow one Polyanthus, it would be well to make it this one. Gold or silver lacing on a red, mahogany or black ground. An absolute gem.
P.'Guinevere' (PO) sometimes listed as 'Garryard Guinevere' bears soft pink flowers over rich bronze-purple foliage.
P.'Midnight' (PO) is a deep blue-black and magenta-purple strain with dark foliage.
P.'Violet Victorians' (PO) may be adequately dark with the colours ranging from violet, purple, plum to bilberry. Blooms have a silken or velvet sheen.
There are also a number of **Wanda hybrids** with dark foliage amongst them is a violet-purple shade with a velvet sheen and little or no eye, rather like a Cowichan. Exceptionally beautiful flowers with gorgeous deeply bronzed foliage.

Of the double primroses **P.vulgaris 'Miss Indigo'** is one of the darkest I have seen. 'Roy Cope' is a very dark crimson.

P.x pubescens 'Hurstwood Midnight' is a hybrid with deep velvety purple-blue flowers suitable for an alpine house.

PRUNUS

Offering some of the best purple foliage and making excellent specimen trees, Prunus are not to be disregarded in the dark-leaf garden. The ones described here are all fully hardy.

CULTIVATION
Moist but well-drained soil is required in full sun.

PROPAGATION
Sow seed of species outdoors in autumn. Root greenwood cuttings of deciduous species in early summer and semi-ripe cuttings of evergreens in midsummer, both with bottom heat. Bud cultivars in summer or graft in early spring.

P.cerasifera 'Nigra' has the most wonderful dark purple foliage which is redder when young and bears flowers of pink. A magnificent, deciduous specimen tree. Can also be used to good effect as a hedge, which needs to be trimmed after flowering. 10m (30ft).
P.cerasifera 'Pissardii' has dark red-purple leaves and pale pink flowers that fade to white.
P.'Fragrant Cloud' ='Shizuka' bears scented, semi-double flowers and bronze foliage.
P.'Royal Burgundy' has impressive deep purple foliage throughout the summer, turning bronze in autumn. A good choice for the small garden, being a sport of 'Kanzan' but less vigorous.
P.cerasifera 'Thundercloud' bears pink flowers and dark purple foliage.
P.spinosa 'Purpurea' the species being the blackthorn or sloe is a dense, spiny deciduous shrub or tree which bears red foliage, later turning dark red-purple. The pale pink flowers contrast admirably with the foliage. 5m (15ft).

The foliage of **P.'Kiku-shidare-zakura'** (synonym Cheal's Weeping') is bronze when young as is that of **P.jamasakura**, and other Prunus species and cultivars. **P.padus 'Colorata'** bears leaves whose new growth is coppery-purple. **P.sargentii** has bronze-red young foliage.

PSEUDERANTHEMUM

Might also be found under Erantherum. A frost tender species grown for its colourful foliage.

CULTIVATION

Under glass, grow in loam-based potting compost in bright filtered light with high humidity. In growth, water moderately, applying a balanced feed every month. Outdoors, grow in humus-rich soil in partial shade. Needs pinching out regularly when young. Cut back hard in spring if they become straggly.Protect from winds. Minimum temperature 13°C (55°F).

PROPAGATION

Root semi-ripe cuttings in midsummer with bottom heat.

P.atropurpureum is an erect, open shrub with deep purple leaves spotted with various colours. Bear tubular white flowers, spotted rose or purple at the bases, during summer. 1-1.5m (3-5ft).
P.atropurpureum 'Variegatum' (syn 'Tricolour') has bronze-purple leaves splashed with creamy yellow and pink. Bears pink flowers.
P.reticulatum has showy foliage varying in colour from green to purplish-black with oval leaves to 15cm (6") netted with golden veins and having wavy margins. In summer, it bears white flowers with cerise markings.

PSEUDOPANAX

Purple leaves on superb foliage plants. Architectural and specimen plants with purple to black fruits. Frost tender.

CULTIVATION

In frost-prone areas grow under glass in loam-based potting compost with added sharp sand, in full light, shaded from hot sun or in bright filtered light. When in growth water moderately, applying a balanced feed every month. Reduce watering in winter.

PROPAGATION

Sow seed in autumn or spring under glass. Take semi-ripe cuttings or air-layer in summer.

P.crassifolius, commonly known as Lancewood, is an evergreen tree which remains unbranched for many years. Mature trees develop a rounded head and palmate foliage. It bears huge, spiky leaves of purplish-red which almost appear black from a distance. Completely hardy in Cornwall. (Burncoose & Southdown).
P.lessonii 'Purpureus' is an erect to spreading large evergreen shrub. Mature foliage is palmate and deep purple. Suitable for a large pot. 3-6m (10-20ft).

PULSATILLA

Beautiful flowers and this one is very rare, but worth waiting for if you can find it.
P.pratensis ssp nigricans is a rare Pulsatilla in which the flower is very dark, almost black.(Mike Hythe). It produces little seed and is always propagated from seed, hence its rarity. Worth seeking.

RANUNCULUS

A wonderful array of dark foliage is provided early in the year, mainly with contrasting yellow flowers. Good for damp soil. Fully hardy.

CULTIVATION
Best in partial or full shade in moist, humus-rich soil. Plant tubers at a depth of 5cm (2").

PROPAGATION
Divide tuberous species in spring or autumn.

R.ficaria 'Aglow in the Dark' was discovered by M.Cragg-Barber. The foliage opens almost black showing very few small pale spots symmetrically placed towards the edge. Ages to dark green.
R.ficaria 'Bitter Chocolate' has leaves of dark green surrounding the central brown bronze zone.
R.ficaria 'Brambling' is a distinct variant with the base colour of the leaf being dull bronze, overlaid with a filigree of silvery lichen green.
R.ficaria 'Brazen Child' is a seedling from 'Brazen Hussy' by R.Hoskins. The dark chocolate leaf is splashed with burgundy red.
R.ficaria 'Brazen Hussy' is a little gem of a plant producing glossy, chocolate-brown to purple leaves and the usual shining golden yellow flower with a bronze reverse. Seedlings often have bronzed leaves. Initially found by Christopher Lloyd. The shiny leaf distinguishes the plant from others of similar colouring.
R.ficaria 'Binsted Woods' is not considered distinct enough to warrant a name of its own, but is said to be a more compact form from Mike Tristram.
R.ficaria 'Burnivale' found by M.Cragg-Barber bears dark, red-purple foliage and

red-purple petioles. Its large and fat tubers are oddly pale white.
R.ficaria 'Coppernob' is a hybrid between R.ficaria 'Brazen Hussy' and R.ficaria v aurantiacus, bearing the foliage of the former with the glowing dark orange flowers of the latter. Another clone is named **R.ficaria 'Brandymount Orange'** a spontaneous cross of the two species.
R.ficaria 'Crawshaw Cream' has dark foliage enhanced by a cream-coloured flower, with a green reverse.
R.ficaria 'Deborah Jope' has bronze leaves admirably set off by single white flowers.
R.ficaria 'Holly Bronze' bears indented bronze leaves.
R.ficaria 'Holly Patchy' has a holly-like shape to the leaves which are irregularly marked bronze.
R.ficaria 'Jane's Dress' found by M.Cragg-Barber bears leaves of purple flecked with silver.
R.ficaria 'Mobled Jade' bears purple-bronze colouring which does not cover the whole of the leaf, the edges bearing green spots and splashes which extend into the darker zone.
R.ficaria 'Molten Lava' is a procumbent form with dark grey bronze leaves with a blue-black sheen and a ring of silvery spots at the periphery. It bears bright yellow flowers marked bright chestnut on the reverse. The plant is smaller than many of the other variants.
R.ficaia 'Newton Abbot' is a wild collected variant found in Devon by C.Rogers which bears leaves of an olive khaki.
R.ficaria 'Suffusion' is similar to **'Mobled Jade'**, having the same spots and splashes but not entering the dark zone to the same extent. Both found by M.Cragg-Barber.
R.ficaria 'Sweet Chocolate' has a chocolate blob surrounded by green.
R.ficaria 'Tortoiseshell' has bold and large foliage with a bronze background wonderfully mottled with shades of green and red. The patterning is variable.

RHODOCHITON

A delightful frost tender perennial not to be missed, can easily climb a screen and make a display in one season.

CULTIVATION
Under glass, grow in loam-based potting compost in full light with shade from hot sun. During growth, water freely, applying a balanced liquid fertiliser monthly. In winter, keep just moist. Pot on in spring. Outdoors grow in fertile, humus-rich, moist but well-drained soil in full sun.

PROPAGATION
Sow seed under glass in spring.

R.atrosanguineus (synonym R.volubilis) is a slender-stemmed twining climber producing rich green heart-shaped leaves 4-8cm long. From summer to autumn, long, pendent stalks bear tubular black to reddish-purple flowers 4.5cm long protruding from cup-shaped, rose-pink to magenta calyces. A delightful climber with quite unusual flowers, which deserves to be grown more. Easy from seed and attractive as an annual climber outdoors in Great Britain. I have seen a suggestion that it can also be used as ground cover, but the effect of the hanging bells would surely be completely lost. In a single season in a conservatory, it can reach 2.6m (8ft). 3m (10ft). A useful climber with interesting flowers which will make a good, quick display when fed and watered well. This is one I would choose to always grow in my garden. It is easy from seed. Minimum temperature 3-5°C (37-41°F).

RHODODENDRON

Some dark flowers and bronzed foliage are available on these well-known shrubs and trees.

R.'Black Hawk' is an Azalea of the deepest crimson-red, flowering May to June.
R.'Black Magic' is a low to medium shrub bearing very dark red flowers in full balled trusses in May to June. Free flowering. Hardy to -5°C. 2m (6ft).
R.'Black Knight' is an evergreen azalea, simply described as red, flowering in May.
R.'Ebony Pearl' is unusual for its maroon leaves, bears pink flowers.

The species **R.sanguineum v sanguinem v haemaleum** bears deep blackish-crimson bells. It will thrive in almost alkaline soil. Hardy to 0°C.

There are also a number of Rhododendrons with bronze leaves when young including **R.'Bow Bells'** with pink flowers, **R.'Cowslip'** with contrasting flowers of primrose to cream and the species **R.lutescens** which is hardy, vigorous and free-flowering. The foliage of the species **R.ovatum** is purple when young with single flowers of mauve.
R.'Elizabeth Lockhart' has new growth of dark chocolate brown.
R.'Moser's Maroon' has striking new leaves of bright red to burgundy with wine-red flowers.
R.'P.J.Mezitt' has mahogany leaves in winter.
R.ponticum 'Foliis Purpureus' has leaves turning purple in winter. Quite rare.
R.'Queen of Hearts' has dark crimson flowers with red stems.

The white flowers of **R.'Sappho'** are marked with purple-black in the throats. Free-flowering.

RICINUS

Architectural, palmate dark leaves make excellent specimen plants. Given the right treatment, they are capable of reaching large proportions in one season. Half hardy.

CULTIVATION
Under glass, grow in loam-based potting compost in full light. Water freely when in growth, applying a balanced feed monthly. Reduce watering in winter. May need restrictive pruning. Outdoors, grow in fertile, humus-rich, well-drained soil in full sun, feed regularly. Plants grown on poor soil will make less vegetative growth and leaves will be smaller.

PROPAGATION
Soak seed for 24 hours before sowing singly in pots under glass in spring. Dislikes root disturbance. Plant out when all danger of frost has passed. Easy from seed. Please note seed is poisonous.

R.communis 'Carmencita' is well-branched with dark, bronze-red foliage and bright red female flowers. Annual growth of 2-3m (6-10ft).

R.communis 'Gibsonii' also bears bronzed foliage.

R.communis 'Impala' is compact with reddish-purple foliage, young shoots and stems being carmine-red. 1.2m (4ft).

R.communis 'Red Spire' is tall with red stems and bronze-flushed leaves.

ROSA

Red roses are the classic symbol of love, make mine the darkest rose, the elusive black beautifully shades some of the darker reds.

CULTIVATION
Tolerant of a wide range of conditions, but preferring an open site in full sun. Thriving in moderately fertile, humus-rich, soil, moist but well-drained.

PROPAGATION
Root hardwood cuttings in autumn. Bud in summer.

R.'Black Beauty' Delbard 1974. The wonderful colouration of rich, crimson scarlet with reflexes of darkest, velvety black. Excellent cutting rose.
R.'Black Ice' is a nearly black rose of R.'Iceberg' parentage! Bearing near black buds, the flowers open to scarlet. (Miss Gandy). Compact. 60cm (2ft).
R.'Black Jack' is a miniature deep red.
R.'Black Prince' bears fragrant, large-cupped flowers of rich carmine shaded almost black. 1866. 1.8m (5ft).
R.'Dark Lady' Austin 1991. Dark red flowers with hints of purple. Not very vigorous.
R.'Deep Secret' Tantau 1979. The darkest of the reds (C & K Jones). Strong, rich fragrance. The perfect blooms are almost black in bud. Exceptional.
R.'Eclair' is a very dark red variety, almost black. Fairly vigorous, free-flowering and scented. Well-formed. 1833.
R.'Josephine Bruce' is the first rose I ever knew the name of at the tender age of 10, it has remained a favourite of mine ever since. Shapely, fully double flowers of a deep velvety red, it is not merely sentiment which makes this rose special. Not the darkest, but lovely nevertheless. As a

climber, its growth is strong, thorny and vigorous, also available as a modern hybrid tea. Scented. Bees 1952. Sometimes, one of the parents is sold under this name, having a weak neck and little scent.

R.'Louis XIV' bears fully double flowers of very dark red almost black, with a good fragrance which is unusual in the China roses. 1859. 60cm (2ft).

R.'Nuits de Young' is said to be the darkest of the old roses. Bears double, scented flowers of a deep purple-maroon with yellow stamens. Erect, compact bush, flowering in early summer. 1.2-1.5m.

R.'Papa Meilland' Meilland 1963. Crimson-red, shading to black, strong fragrance.

R.'Prince Camille de Rohan' bears very deep, blackish-red blooms of almost colossal size on a vigorous plant that unfortunately has a rather weak neck. 120cm. (4ft).

R.rubrifolia is a species wild rose bearing probably the best wine-coloured foliage, particularly on the undersides. The flowers are red at first, then greenish-white. Profuse number of hips in autumn. Makes a good hedge. Naturalises readily from seed. (See other reddish foliage opposite).

R.'Ruby Celebration' Pearce 1995. A red so dark that you can almost see black shading. Flowers are smallish and plentiful.

R.'Tuscany Superb' is a large gallica, bearing semi-double blooms of the deepest velvety crimson, emphasised by prominent gold stamens. Strongly scented, erect and well foliated. Pre 1848.

Confronted with so many dark red beauties, and given the subjectiveness of colour, it is difficult to maintain the perfect vision, so here are some other dark roses you might like to consider. R.'Charles Mallerin', R.'Crimson Glory', R.'Deep Secret', the delightful floribunda R.'Dusky Maiden', R.'Gipsy Boy' a lovely Bourbon,

R.'Marchioness of Salisbury', the dark buds and flowers of R.'Roudelay' or the rich velvety burgundy-purple flowers of the gallica R.'Cardinal de Richelieu' the deep beetroot purple of R.'Big Purple', or red turning to purple of R.'The Prince'. Of the climbers R.'Guinee' is a very dark blackish-red with fully-cupped double flowers and 'R.'Jazz' is also dark red.

Rosa pimpinellifolia could be used in the dark garden for a different reason. It bears creamy-white flowers which are followed by blackish hips. R. 'Single Cherry' has the same coloured hips.

Roses of other colours, often bear foliage of bronze or red.

The new growth of R.'Bride' is a distinctive shiny red, that of R.'Eternally Yours' and of R.'Too Hot to Handle' is bronze-red whilst R.'Kathryn McGredy' bears glorious plum-red new growth as does R.'Paddy Stephens'. The new growth of R.'Oranges and Lemons' is a glossy red turning dark green as it ages.

The striking young foliage of R.'The Painter' is a glossy reddish bronze which ages to dark green, and shading to the same colour but beginning bronze-reddish is R.'Panache', whilst that of R.'Piccolo' is a glossy reddish colour.

R.'Ice Cream' is clothed in bronzy green foliage, likewise R.'Arcadian' and also R.'Edith Holden', that of R.'Hannah Gordon' being a glossy bronze-green. R.'Lovers Meeting' bears deep bronze foliage as do R.'Firefly', R.'Solitaire' and R.'Regensburg'. R.'Thank You' bears lovely bronze foliage.

The new foliage of R.'Fiesta' is shaded red. R.'English Miss' bears purplish to dark green foliage and R.'Gordon's College' bears purplish tinted young foliage.

R.'Brown Velvet' bred by Sam McGredy in 1983 is a lovely shade of russet brown with reddish shadings and bronze foliage.

RUDBECKIA

Most Rudbeckias have black central cones to their daisy flowers, but this one is a little more unusual.

CULTIVATION
Grow in moderately fertile soil which does not dry out in full sun or partial shade.

PROPAGATION
Sow seed in a cold frame in early spring, or divide in autumn or spring.

R.occidentalis 'Green Wizard' is a curiously interesting plant with a stop you in your tracks look. Bright green sepals surround the dark green to black conical centre providing a superb contrast. Perfect for dynamic flower arranging. 1m (3ft).

SALPIGLOSSIS

An annual or short-lived perennial to add to your chocolate collection. Half hardy.

CULTIVATION
Under glass grow in loamless or loam-based compost in full light with shade from hot sun. Requires low to high humidity when in growth. Apply a balanced liquid fertiliser every 2 weeks. Keep just moist in winter at a temperature of 17°C (62°F).

PROPAGATION
Sow seed under glass in mid-spring or in autumn or late winter for early flowering pot plants.

S.'Chocolate Royale' (synonym 'Chocolate Pot') is compact with an elegant branching habit. Produces masses of rich, chocolate-brown, veined trumpet flowers with a velvet sheen. 30cm (12").

SALVIA

With over 900 species, the Salvias have something dark to offer in flower and foliage. Fully hardy to frost tender.

CULTIVATION
Outdoors, grow in light, moderately fertile, humus-rich, moist but well-drained soil in full sun or light dappled shade. Tender varieties need protection from winter wet as well as frost and can be raised under glass.

PROPAGATION
Can be raised from seed, hardy varieties in a cold frame in spring. Annuals in mid-spring under glass.

S.discolor is a tender perennial with densely white-woolly branched stems, leaves the same underneath, but less hairy on the surface. Bears racemes of deep indigo-black flowers to 2.5cm (1") with finely white-hairy calyces in summer to early autumn. 45cm (18").
S.guaranitica 'Black and Blue' (syn. S.caerulea h) is a subshrubby tender perennial bearing rich blue flowers with very dark purple calyces. 2.5m (8ft).
S.officinalis Purpurascens Group has red-purple young leaves. A subshrubby, evergreen hardy perennial with aromatic leaves to 8cm (3") long. 1m .
Depending on how strict you wish to be in your dark garden, you could find other Salvias that will suit. **S.cacaliifolia** is another tender species of deepest blue. **S.farinacea 'Rhea' and 'Victoria'** are dark intense blues or **S.greggii 'Desert Blaze'** with maroon-scarlet flowers. **S.x sylvestris 'Mainacht'** has intense blue-purple flowers from dark, almost black stems or the burgundy-leaved **S.lyrata 'Burgundy Bliss'** would make a superb addition to any garden.

SAMBUCUS

Increasingly darker cultivars of S.nigra are making their way on to the market. Fully hardy.

CULTIVATION
Moderately fertile, humus-rich, moist but well-drained soil in full sun or dappled shade. Can be pruned hard to restrict size.

PROPAGATION
Take hardwood cuttings in winter. Take greenwood cuttings in early summer.

S.nigra 'Black Beauty' is now considered to be the darkest elder available. The dark, almost black foliage is combined with lemon-scented pink flowers in June, followed by berries in autumn. Will reach a height of up to 3m (10ft) in eight years if left unpruned, when it should make a good free-standing specimen, or can be cut back hard like other elders at the end of each season. Part of a breeding programme which promises to introduce more new varieties in the near future.

S.nigra 'Guincho Purple' was long considered the darkest black elder. Bearing dark green leaves which turn a blackish-purple then red in autumn, purple-stalks and pink-tipped flowers. Prune hard, good in the herbaceous border. 6m (20ft).

S.nigra 'Thundercloud' is a mutation from S. nigra 'Guincho' whose dark red-black leaves colour best in full sun and is perhaps a little darker. The red-pink flowers are startling in May-June.

SANGUISORBA

Dark reddish-purple or maroon small bottlebrush flowers can be found on some Burnets. Fully hardy.

CULTIVATION
Grow in moderately fertile retentive soil which does not dry out in full sun or partial shade. Taller species may require staking. Sometimes invasive.

PROPAGATION
Sow seed in a cold frame in spring or autumn or divide established clumps at the same time.

S.menziesii has deep maroon bottlebrush flowers from May to July over pinnate foliage. 60cm (2ft).

S.officinalis bears pinnate basal leaves with red-brown to maroon flowers borne on red stems from early summer to mid-autumn. 1.2m (4ft).

S.officinalis 'Shiro Fururin' produces broad serrated leaves with a sparkling white variegated edge, and burgundy flowers from June to July. 60cm (2ft).

S.officinalis 'Tanna' is a well-behaved dwarf version of the Great Burnet which has burgundy- maroon flowers arising on spikes to 30cm (12") from June - September. A neat, compact plant of 25cm (14") Perfect front-of-the-border plant.

S.tenuifolia 'Purpurea' bears tall maroon-purple spikes from August to October. 1.2m (4ft).

SAUROMATUM

Not everything, even in the plantworld, can be beautiful, and this is one black plant I do not like. It is another malodourous plant with no redeeming beauty. Frost tender.

CULTIVATION

Tubers should be planted at a depth of 15cm (6") in late winter. Under glass, grow in loam-based compost in bright filtered or indirect light. Water moderately when in growth. Keep completely dry in winter. Tubers are capable of flowering on a saucer without soil or water. Outdoors grow in well-drained, fertile, humus-rich, neutral to slightly acid soil in partial shade.

PROPAGATION

Remove offsets when dormant in winter.

S.venosum, the Voodoo lily is a tuberous perennial producing a yellowish or greenish-white spathe which is heavily spotted with purple from which arises a foul-smelling , greenish-purple spadix in spring and early summer. The spathe is followed by a single leaf. Minimum temperature 5°C (41°F).

This was unsuspectingly sold to me four years ago as a black plant by a well known nursery in the Cotswolds. I would not have bought it, had I seen it in flower first.

SAXIFRAGA

A large genus varying in habit and leaf form with different cultural requirements, offering interest for the dark garden. Fully hardy.

PROPAGATION

Sow seed in autumn in an open frame. Divide herbaceous perennials in spring. Detach rosettes in late spring or summer.

S.'Blackberry and Apple Pie' (fortunei) has green foliage spotted dark and the undersides being bright red. 15cm (6").

S.'Black Ruby'(fortunei) (synonym 'Black Leaf', black leaf form) is another of the new introductions from Japan and perhaps a most valuable addition to the dark garden with very dark almost black stems and leaves. Bearing red-pink flowers from October to December. A glossy plant requiring moist shade and good soil, colours best in deep shade. 15cm (6").

S.fortunei variegated also new from Japan and of marginal interest to the dark garden has foliage well speckled with pink and white and purple on the underside. 15cm.

S.'Maroon Beauty' (stolonifera) large evergreen, maroon marked leaves for dry shade under trees. 30cm (12").

S.'Miss Chambers' (x urbium) bears stately crimson flowers in April-June with darker maroon-green leaves. 30cm (12").

S.'Rokujo' (fortunei) has red and brown leaves with contrasting white flowers from September to November. 25cm (8").

S.'Rubrifolia' (fortunei) is a choice plant for cool soil in a sheltered position. A compact plant bearing round, varnished leaves, suffused deep red on the surface, carmine on the underside. In October white sprays of flowers are borne on the red stems. 30cm.

S.'Velvet' (fortunei) is another dark-leaved form.

S.'Wada' (fortunei) bears very large glossy, coppery leaves, red on the underside, with clouds of white flowers. 50cm (20").

S.'Wisley' (frederici-augusti ssp grisebachii) has a pleasing dark reddish-maroon flower over spoon-shaped silver-grey leaves. The arching pink stems are clothed in green-tipped reddish-purple bracts. 10cm (4").

SCABIOSA

One of my favourite flowers for their almost black buds, opening to velvety maroon. Fully hardy.

CULTIVATION

This plant goes under several names, and I suspect they are all one and the same, but it is often classified as an anuual, biennial or perennial! Having grown it I would say it is a biennial, possibly short-lived perennial under favourable conditions. In my garden it does not self-seed, under dry,warmer conditions it may do so. Moderately fertile, well-drained, neutral to slightly alkaline soil in full sun. Protect from excessive winter wet.

PROPAGATION

Sow seed in early spring under glass or in situ mid-spring.

S.'Chile Black' (synonyms 'Ace of Spades', 'Black Prince' and 'Satchmo'). I first had it as 'Satchmo' and it was superbly black, especially in bud. From a basal rosette of toothed leaves, arises a long stem in the second year, bearing solitary blackish buds, opening to astounding scabious flowers of a deep dark velvety maroon black-red borne throughout summer. Stunning and easy from seed. 60cm (2ft +).

SCOLIOPUS

Grown for their unusual but malodorous flowers, the tender Stink Pod might not be quite what you are looking for in the dark garden.

CULTIVATION

Requires humus-rich, leafy, moist but well-drained, acid to neutral soil in deep to partial shade. Will benefit from a dry winter mulch. Suitable for alpine house.

PROPAGATION

Sow seed when fresh.

S.bigelovii is a compact herbaceous perennial with attractive dull, dark green leaves which are mottled purple. In early spring, bears umbels of 3-12 trillium-like flowers to 5cm (2") across. They display narrow, erect deep purple inner tepals and greenish white outer tepals, striped brown-purple. 10cm (4").

SCOPOLIA

Dark pendent bells on a woodland plant. Die back after flowering. Fully hardy.

CULTIVATION

Humus-rich, leafy, moist but very well-drained, neutral to slightly alkaline soil in partial shade.

PROPAGATION

Sow seed in a cold frame in autumn, or in situ in autumn or spring. Divide in spring.

The species **S.carniolica** is a creeping, rhizomatous perennial with ovate to ovate-oblong, pointed, veined and wrinkled leaves to 15cm (6") long. Solitary 5-pointed, bell-shaped, brownish purple to red flowers 2.5cm (1"). long, yellow-green inside are borne from the leaf axils in mid and late spring. 60cm (2ft).

S.carniolica 'Zwanenburg' carries drooping deep purple (of a much deeper colour than the species) bells from March to May. 30cm (1ft).

All parts are toxic if ingested.

SEDUM

Red or purple tinted foliage can be found on quite a number of Sedums and there have been more than a few new introductions. Attractive fleshy leaves. Fully hardy.

CULTIVATION
Grow in moderately fertile, well-drained, neutral to slightly alkaline soil in full sun. Excessive moisture, overfeeding and too much shade affect the colouring and habit of Sedums from S.telephium ssp maximum 'Atropurpureum' parentage.

PROPAGATION
Sow seed in containers in autumn. Divide in spring. Take softwood cuttings of non-flowering shoots in early summer.

S.'Arthur Branch' a well-established dark chocolate foliage and blood-red stemmed favourite has been outclassed by S.'Lynda et Rodney', see below.

S.'Bertram Anderson', long a favourite of mine. Bears stunning black leaves on slightly lax stems and deep pink flowers from August to October. 15cm (6").

S.'El Cid' is similar to 'Lynda et Rodney' see below.

S.'Joyce Henderson' is similar to 'Matrona' but looser and lax in habit, there is a mottling on the foliage.

S.'Purple Emperor' has matt purple foliage which is very deep at the time of flowering. Purplish-pink flowers. Best kept on the dry side for an intensely-coloured, compact, upright plant. 45cm (18").

S.'Ruby Glow' has soft grey-purple leaves with ruby red flowers. 50cm (20").

S.'Strawberries and Cream' has dark foliage, pale flowers and a rather lax habit.

S.'Sunset Cloud' has dark glaucous foliage and rich, wine-purple flowers.

S.telephium 'Leonore Zuutz' bears very dark blue-black foliage which is narrower than usual. Open sprays of pale-pinky flowers. 50cm (20").

S.telephium ssp. telephium 'Lynda et Rodney' is one to look out for - a wild find by Frenchman Jean-Pierre Jolivot and named after Lynda Windsor and Rodney Davey of RD Plants in Devon. Bears narrow brownish-purple foliage, red stems and tight, domed heads of flowers with pale pinkish-purple petals and strawberry-red ovaries, both of which darken with age. Taller than others from this parentage, it reaches a height of 80cm (32"). Recently chosen by Alan Leslie as the pick of the bunch. Lynda tells me they have been making selections from this and there will be an even darker foliage plant released in 2001, **S.'Lynda Windsor'** bears almost black, bitter chocolate foliage with glowing dark claret flowers. Stunningly dark and tall. Plant Breeders Rights apply. An exciting plant that will not disappoint.

S.telephium 'Matrona' is a German seedling of large and luxuriant proportions. Thick, succulent stems rise to 60cm (24"), kept in sun and in moderate soil they will remain strong and erect, overfed, they have a tendency to become weak and lax. The leaves are greyish-green in spring becoming suffused with purple as summer progresses. Pink flowerheads are borne in August and September.

S.telephium'Mohrchen' is of S.telephium ssp telephium parentage with dark foliage and flowers.

S.telephium 'Munstead Red' has purple-tinted dark green leaves and dark purplish red flowers, becoming darker with age. Makes a continuous attractive show into autumn, with flowers at various stages in colours of raspberry red through to deep bronze.

S.telephium subspecies maximum 'Atropurpureum' has dark purple, thick fleshy leaves and stems, but the cultivars supersede it even though it makes a good dark accent plant. Chocolate-brown seedheads will add interest later in the year. 45cm (18").

Bob Brown of Cotswold Garden Flowers has a purple leaf form which may be the same as the Washfield purple selection, of a darker shade than the above.

S.'Veluwe se Wakel' is similar to 'Lynda et Rodney'.

S.'Vera Jameson' bears dusky pink flowers on arching grey-pink branches. 25cm.

The following are not as dark as the Sedums of telephium parentage, but are pleasing additions to the garden.

S.spathulifolium 'Purpureum' is a vigorous, evergreen perennial, producing leaves which are richly suffused reddish purple to wine-red in a good form. 10cm (4").

S.spurium 'Purpurteppich' (syn 'Purple Carpet) is compact with deep plum-purple leaves and dark purplish red flowers. 10cm (4").

S.spurium 'Schorbluser Blut' (synonym 'Dragon's Blood') has green leaves which are purple-tinted when mature. Bears deep pink flowers. 10cm (4").

The following might also be of interest.

S.aizoon 'Euphorbioides' has bronzy leaves and bronzy flowers followed by handsome seedheads from June to October.(Bob Brown) no-one else mentions anything about bronze on this. 30cm (12").

S.obtusatum (syn S.rubroglacum) bears rosettes of mid-green leaves, flushed crimson in autumn.

S.rubrotinctum bears arching, rooting stems of mid-green leaves which are often flushed red.

S.spectabile 'Indian Chief' has flat heads of maroon flowers.

S.spectabile 'Meteor' bears purple flowerheads from August to October.

SEMPERVIVUM

Evergreen succulents with thick, fleshy, pointed leaves which are often very dark. Fully hardy.

CULTIVATION

Grow in poor to moderately fertile, sharply drained soil with added grit in full sun.

PROPAGATION

Sow seed in a cold frame in spring. Rosettes die after flowering, so root offsets in spring or early summer.

S.'Black Claret', 'Black Mini', S.'Black Mountain', S.'Black Prince' and **S.'Black Velvet'** would all suggest by their names that they are the darkest, near black houseleeks.

S.'Black Knight' is mahogany purple with red tips and forms tight rosettes.

S.'Dark Beauty' has very dark rosettes.

S.'Gravpurpur' bears reddish-bronze leaves.

S.'Jungle Fires' is similar to 'Quintessence' but the leaves are more pointed and the green edging extends further into the darker purple main colour of the plant.

S.'Quintessence' has deep reddish-purple leaves with green tips. Very attractive.

S.'Red Devil' has very dark, tightly packed rosettes.

S.'Rotkopf' produces large rosettes of a dusky dark purple.

There are many more to look out for including S.'Aarlrica', S.'Atropurpureum', S.'Bellott's Pourpre', S.'Bladon', S,'Cavo Doro', S.'Cherry Tart', S.'Congo', S.'Damask', S.'Dark Cloud', S.'Darkie', S.'Dark Point', S.'Dark Fire' , S.'Hayling', S.'Night Raven', S.'Othello', S.'Purple King', S.'Red Indian', S.'Red Shadows', S.'Rouge', S.'Shawnee', S.'Starburst', S.'Vanbalen' , S.'Virgil' and S.'Zeppherin'.

SOLENOSTEMON

Referred to by most under the name of Coleus, this genus produces dramatic foliage plants for summer bedding or as houseplants. Frost tender.

CULTIVATION

Under glass, grow in loam-based potting compost in bright filtered or moderate light. Water freely, applying a high-nitrogen fertiliser every two weeks during the growing season. Keep just moist in winter. Pot on annually in spring. Outdoors, grow in humus-rich, moist but well-drained soil, enriched with well-rotted organic matter. A sheltered position is preferred in full sun or partial shade. Water freely in dry weather. Pinch out young shoots to prevent straggly growth. For best foliage, remove flowers.

PROPAGATION

Surface sow seed under glass in early spring for summer bedding or anytime for use as houseplants. A decent plant can be had in 3 months. Root softwood cuttings with bottom heat in spring or summer. Though not ideal, roots easily in water.

S.'Atlas' bears very large, cupped leaves, flame patterns and a purple border which can be pink or violet.

S.'Black Dragon' produces a riot of frilled and crested leaves of deep purple to maroon-black around a raised medallion flecked pink or violet . Colour holds well in winter.

S.'Black Magic' is a modestly statured plant of upright habit with mahogany purple dragon leaves outlined in avocado scallops with a lime-encircled central raised medallion.

S.'Black Night' has widely fingered pine green leaves with purplish maroon designs surrounding the central raised medallion veined violet.

S.'Black Prince' is a self-coloured almost black foliage plant. Stunning.

S.'Brocade' is a deep magenta purple.

S.'Bronze Pagoda' bears bronzy chartreuse wide leaves with a central blood-red spattering and soft violet veins.

S.'Burgundy Columns' has burnt-red to purple foliage.

S.'Cantigny Royale' bears elaborately lobed mahogany-maroon leaves tightly packed on much branched stems.

S.'Chocolate Bingo' is a dusky olive and pistachio green, modulating into chocolate purple crenated margins.

S.'Dark Frills' is a sport of S.'Indian Frills' with a very dark, dramatic centre.

S.'Dark Star' is perhaps one of the darkest of all. Bearing black-purple wide leaves, closely spaced on branching ebony-violet stems. Has very flat foliage.

S.'Ella Cinders' has dark olive designs which are never repeating on dusky purple trim foliage. The colour changes in different light.

S.'Jupiter' is a compact 'Molten Fire' with tiny furled finger leaves of deep blackish mahogany-purple edged avocado.

S.'Molten Lava' is an incredible combination of red-hot lava centre surrounded by black edges. Foliage is extremely crimped and crinkled. Stunning. Available from seed.

S.'Othello' bears deep purple-black leaves which are richly fluted. Smaller and darker than 'Jupiter'.

S.'Palisandra' available from seed is a definite contender for the darkest of all. Self-colour which is almost black, slight purple hint to it, lush, velvety rich broad leaves. Similar to and could be a seed version of S. 'Black Prince'. 45cm (18").

S.'Purple Emperor' is a lovely plant bearing large, velvety deep purple-black leaves with wavy, scalloped edges and is of vigorous growth.

STREPTOCARPUS

The Cape Primroses are delightful plants with sumptuous flowers offering the deepest purples. Frost tender.

CULTIVATION

Under glass, grow in loamless potting compost in bright filtered light. Shade from hot sun, indoors grow on an east or west facing windowsill. When in growth, water freely allowing compost to dry out between waterings. Apply a high potash fertiliser every two weeks. Reduce humidity and watering in winter, keeping just moist and frost free. Repot annually in spring, and gradullay commence watering and feeding. Keep slightly pot bound for the best flowers, with the correct treatment you can achieve flowering from May into winter. Remove faded flowers and stalks. Outdoors, grow in fertile, leafy, humus-rich soil which is moist but well-drained in partial shade.

PROPAGATION

Surface sow seed in late winter or spring. Divide or take leaf cuttings in spring to early summer. Root stem-tip cuttings in spring with bottom heat.

S.'Black Panther' is an American variety with the deepest purple flowers, with blackish hints. Two thin yellow bars emerge from the centre of the throat. Contrasts perfectly with the fresh green primrose-like foliage.

S.'Anne' introduced in 1993 has the same deepest purple colour flowers as one of its parents S.'Elsi', but has the distinction of bearing fully double flowers.

S.'Elsi' is a spectacular colour with large flowers of the deepest purple with two small yellow flashes at the centre.

SYMPLOCARPUS

An American native plant, S.foetidus is usually listed as the only species, but I recently received information on the species below, almost never seen in cultivation, from an American friend. Frost hardy.

CULTIVATION

Grow in rich, moist, very retentive or wet soil in sun or light dappled shade.

PROPAGATION

S.foetidus is normally grown from seed, obtain fresh seed if possible, the tubers are difficult to divide.

S.foetidus produces purple-brown flowers before the leaves appear. They exude a strong, unpleasant smell when bruised. The flowers are not too pleasant smelling either, being pollinated by ground beetles. This plant will not be to everyone's taste.

S.nipponicus is a dwarf Japanese skunk cabbage which is very rare in cultivation. A miniature version of the American native species, it grows to about a quarter of the size. The nearly black flowers are produced in spring.

TACCA

Bizarre is perhaps the word most often chosen to describe this genus, but the flowers have a beauty all of their own and they are dark. Frost tender.

CULTIVATION
Under glass, grow in equal parts of leaf mould and coarse bark with added slow-release fertiliser in bright filtered light. Water freely in summer, reducing in winter and mist regularly in summer. Apply a half strength foliar feed monthly. Pot on every 2 to 3 years and remove old, decaying rhizomes. Outdoors, grow in fertile, moist but well-drained, leafy, acid soil in partial shade. Minimum temperature 13°C (55°F).

PROPAGATION
Surface sow seed in spring. Requires a high temperature and can be erratic and slow. Takes two to three years to flower from seed. Divide in spring.

T.chantrieri, commonly known as the bat plant, cat's whiskers or devil flower, is an unusual flower. The common names conjure up an image of something malevolent and evil, but the flowers are curiously beautiful. It is an erect, rhizomatous perennial with oblong or lance-shaped green leaves. In summer, it bears 5-petalled flowers of black, brown and green each with 2 pairs of black, brown or green floral bracts and black or maroon thread-like whiskers to 25cm (10") long. Reaches a height of 1m (3ft).

T.integrifolia is similar bearing purple-red or brown flowers, with 4 deep purple or green floral bracts and thread-like whiskers are suffused violet and darken with age. 1.2m (4ft).

TELLIMA

Herbaceous perennials providing purple or bronze leaves, suitable for ground cover in shady shrub gardens or woodland. Fully hardy.

CULTIVATION
Moist, humus-rich soil in partial shade, will tolerate dry soil and full-sun. Self-seeds freely.

PROPAGATION
Sow seed in a cold frame when fresh or in spring. Divide in spring.

T.grandiflora Rubra Group (synonym 'Purpurea') bears evergreen leaves which are purple on the underside, green on the surface, turning reddish-purple to bronze in autumn and winter. In early summer, pink-fringed, green bells are borne on long spikes. 50cm (20").

T.grandiflora 'Purpurteppich' is an improvement on the above with tougher leaves colouring maroon purple earlier in the year and holding their colour well. Pink stained rims to green bell flowers on dark stems in spring. 50cm (20").

TIARELLA

Attractive, woodland herbaceous perennials offering some bronzed foliage. Fully hardy.

CULTIVATION
Tolerate a wide range of conditions, but prefer cool, moist, humus-rich soil in deep or partial shade. Dislike excessive winter wet.

PROPAGATION
Sow seed in a cold frame in spring or when fresh. Divide in spring.

T.'Dark Eyes' bears glossy leaves with a dark central blotch and spikes of beige flowers from April to June. 30cm (12").
T.'Inkblot' has large dark markings which develop on mature leaves. Spikes of pinkish flowers from April to June or later. Suitable even in dry shade. 30cm (12").
T.'Mint Chocolate' has maple-shaped leaves with a brown central blotch, and pinkish flowers. Makes excellent ground cover. 30cm (12").
T.'Ninja' makes good ground cover even in dry shade. It bears maple shaped leaves with a brown overlay turning blackish-purple, especially in winter and coral-beige flowers in spring. 30cm (12").
T.'Tiger Stripe' makes neat clumps of green, crimped leaves each with a maroon-brown centre veining outwards. Pink spires of flowers on slender stems from May to August. Semi to full shade. 20cm (8").
T.wherryi 'Bronze Beauty' is a compact perennial, slowly making a clump of dark red-bronze foliage and light pinkish white flowers from March to December. An older, much admired variety. 20cm (8").

The green leaves of **T.polyphylla** are veined brown.

TORENIA

A cheeky gem of an annual with delightful flowers. The wishbone flower is frost tender.

CULTIVATION
Under glass, grow in loam-based potting compost in bright, filtered light, providing good ventilation. Water freely when in growth, applying a high-potash liquid fertiliser every 2 or 3 weeks. Pinch out stem tips for bushy plants. Outdoors, grow in fertile, moist but well-drained soil in partial shade. Grow as a houseplant or in a greenhouse. Minimum temperature 5°C (41°F).

PROPAGATION
Easy from seed sown in mid-spring. Harden off and plant out after danger of frost has passed.

T.fournieri is an erect annual with toothed pale green leaves. In summer it produces showy flowers of lilac-purple with deeper purple lower lips, the throats being marked with yellow. 30cm (12").
The deep purple can also be found in the mixture known as the Clown Series.

I like to use the darkest to fill gaps at the front of the border, flowers are fairly small, so they can get lost amongst taller plants. Also good for containers.

TRADESCANTIA

Fleshy purple-flushed leaves and attractive flowers make Tradescantias worth growing. Ideal for hanging baskets. Fully hardy to frost tender.

CULTIVATION
Under glass, grow in loam-based or loamless potting compost in bright filtered light. Water moderately in active growth, applying a balanced liquid feed every month. Reduce watering in winter. Pinch out to encourage bushy plants. Pot on each spring. Outdoors, grow in moist, fertile soil in full sun or partial shade. Tender species need a minimum temperature of 10-16°C (50-61°F).

PROPAGATION
Take stem tip cuttings of tender Tradescantias at any time, root in cuttings compost or water. Divide hardy species and cultivars in autumn or spring.

T.pallida 'Purpurea' (syn. 'Purple Heart') is a tender, trailing perennial. Stems are purple and the pointed fleshy leaves are a rich violet-purple. In summer, contrasting pink flowers are borne. Leaves produce their best colour in bright sunlight, with the root zone slightly dry and cramped. Attractive. 20cm (8").

The leaves of **T.spathacea** are green above and purple on the underside. White flowers are surrounded by prominent, long-lasting purple bracts throughout the year. Tender, semi-erect perennial. 30cm (12").

T.zebrina 'Purpusii' is a tender, trailing perennial bearing rich bronze-purple leaves and pink flowers. The leaf colour is usually better on the underside. 15cm (6").

TRIFOLIUM

The ornamental clovers as opposed to the invasive weed have interestingly dark foliage. Fully hardy.

CULTIVATION
Grow in moist, but well-drained neutral soil in full sun. Ideal in containers, or capable of making good ground cover.

PROPAGATION
Sow seed in a cold frame in spring. Divide or detach and replant rooted stems in spring.

T.repens 'Purple Velvet' (syn. pratense 'Chocolate') is a more purple-brown leaved form.
T.repens 'Purpurascens' is a chocolate brown clover with small white flowers. 10cm (4").
T.repens 'Quadrifolium Purpurascens' as above, but four-leaved.
T.repens 'Wheatfen' is an exotic deep red clover with good-sized white flowers. Excellent in containers.

WANT TO GROW POTENTIALLY INVASIVE PLANTS?

Not sure how some plants will behave in the garden? Plant them up in containers and keep a close eye on their habits, you will soon know if a plant is safe to put out in the garden or best kept under the restraint of a container.
Do not feed excessively and watch for bad habits.
If you are happy enough to plant the suspect out in the garden, you can still make efforts to contain it. Surround the roots with slates or to be absolutely safe simply plunge the pot with the plant in it, into the garden.

TRILLIUM

Ideal for the shady border or woodland garden, Trilliums will not fail to please with their attractive foliage and dark flowers. Fully hardy.

CULTIVATION

Grow in deep humus-rich soil, moist but well-drained preferably acid to neutral soil. Deep or partial shade is most suitable. Mulch annually with leaf mould in autumn.

PROPAGATION

Sow fresh seed in a shaded cold frame. Leaves normally appear in the second spring and plants take 5-7 years to reach flowering size. Divide rhizomes after flowering, ensuring each section has at least one growing point, may be slow to re-establish.

T.cuneatum sometimes confused with the species below, differs in its leaves being longer and although marbled, it does not usually have maroon markings. The musk-scented, dark-maroon flowers have olive sepals. Seedlings are variable. 45cm (18").
T.decumbens is a fine, American wildflower, with mottled grey leaves that lie flat on the ground. Bears showy, red-purple flowers. Easy in shade.
T.erectum bears deep red-purple flowers. 50cm (20").
T.recurvatum has mottled green leaves with deep maroon flowers, with strongly recurving green sepals. 40cm (16").
T.sessile bears attractive marbled deep green leaves, the marbling often including bronze-maroon. Stalkless, upright, red-maroon flowers are borne above the leaves in late spring. 30cm (12").
T.underwoodii bears leaves mottled dark purple and grey. Bears red-purple flowers. 25cm (10").

Most of the above can be variable producing other coloured flowers too and are best seen in bloom before you buy. You could also look out for **T.angustipetalum, T.decipiens, T.gracile, T.kurabayashii, T.reliquum, T.stamineum** or **T.sulcatum** which can all produce dark flowers.

TROPAEOLUM

Although perhaps the darkest Nasturtiums you will find, I think to name them black is a misnomer and leads to disappointment, but it does demonstrate that you must not just buy everything that has black in its name.

CULTIVATION

Annual Nasturtiums are easy to look after since they are so undemanding. They prefer poor soil, on rich soils they produce leaves at the expense of flowers. T.majus described below is frost tender.

PROPAGATION

Sow seed under glass in early spring or in situ mid-spring. Children will enjoy growing these. Insert seeds in any vacant spot, where you need a trailing plant.

T. 'Black Jack' bears deep-blue leaves and carmine-red flowers.
T.'Black Prince' is similar and is probably the same variety.
T.'Empress of India' is a dwarf, bushy annual with purple-green leaves bearing semi-double velvety rich scarlet flowers from summer to autumn.
T.'Vesuvius' is also on offer, described as an old cultivar, the two blacks seem to have disappeared from the seed catalogues. Again, it is not really dark - bluish-green leaves, and flowers in shades of salmon or salmon-pink, each with a dark spot on the base of the upper petals.

TULIPA

Bulbs with the most elegant cup-shaped flowers and very dark indeed. Perfect combination for white or pink and a welcome addition to the dark garden. Fully hardy.

CULTIVATION
Grow in fertile, well-drained soil in full sun, sheltered from strong winds. Dislike exessive wet. Plant at a depth of 10-15cm (4-6"). Bulbs are best planted in November.

PROPAGATION
Separate offsets after lifting in summer.

T.'Arabian Mystery' is a fairly dark purple with a narrow feathered white margin. 50cm (20").
T.'Black Parrot' is dark chocolate, maroon-purple and frilled at the margins of the petals. Excellent with T.'White Parrot'. 55cm (22").
T.'Havran' is maroon-black and can bear 2-3 flowers per stem. 45cm (18").
T.'Queen of Night' produces single, velvety dark maroon flowers in late spring. Beautiful, stunning and still the darkest. Appear purple with the light behind them, otherwise very near black. The petals have a silky sheen. Excellent with T.'Purissima'. Look out for a double form **T.'Uncle Tom'** 60cm (24").
T.humilis, offering cultivars with purple flowers and black bases to the petals.
T.humilis 'Odalisque' described as pale purple or as beetroot purple (Jacques Amand) may be worth considering. 10cm (4").
T. humilis v pulchella Violacea Group black base bears deepish violet flowers each with a black base to the petals.10cm. There was also a cultivar named **T.'Black Diamond'** in circulation about 10 years ago, where is it now?

TYPHA

The bulrush was one of my favourites as a child. Marginal aquatics which provide excellent heads for drying. Fully hardy.

CULTIVATION
Grow in water 30-40cm (12-16") deep. Needs plenty of room for root growth. Pick flowerheads for drying early in the season.

PROPAGATION
Divide rootstock in spring.

T.latifolia , the bulrush has strap-shaped leaves to 2m (6ft) or more and bears dark brown flower spikes. 2m (6ft) or more with an indefinite spread.

UNCINIA

Tufted reddish-bronze grasses, preferring damp or moist soil. Frost hardy, tolerate temperatures to about -10°C (14°F) for short periods.

CULTIVATION
Grow in moderately fertile, humus-rich, moist soil in full sun or light dappled shade. In frost prone areas, grow in a sheltered site and mulch in winter.

PROPAGATION
Sow seed under glass in spring. Divide any time from late spring to midsummer. Can self seed mildly.

U.rubra is an evergreen tufted perennial with short rhizomes. It bears abruptly pointed sharp leaves of a greenish red to brown and dark brown to black flowers. 30cm (12").
U.unciniata is smaller with reddish-brown leaves and brown flowers. 25cm (10").

VERATRUM

Almost black flowers on an imposing plant. Does have a white counterpart. Fully hardy.

CULTIVATION
Grow in deep, fertile, moist but well-drained soil with added, well-rotted organic matter. Choose a site in partial shade or in full sun where the soil is still retentive and will not dry out. Provide shelter from cold winds.

PROPAGATION
Sow fresh seed in containers in a cold frame. Veratrum seedlings develop very slowly and take many years to flower. Divide in autumn or early spring.

V.nigrum is a rhizomatous perennial with pleated long basal leaves and few stem leaves. The black rhizomes are poisonous. Leaves are hairless on the surface, but hairy-veined on the underside. In mid to late summer unpleasantly scented , star-shaped flowers are borne in terminal panicles of up to 45cm (18") long of a reddish-brown to nearly black colour with green striped backs. Fabulous foliage and a plume of maroon stars. 120cm (2-4ft).

Please note all parts are highly toxic if ingested.

VIOLA

Surely the cheekiest plants and black suits them immensely. Violas and pansies are some of the prettiest little plants for the garden, much used in bedding schemes, containers or as fillers and ideal for black and white contrast. Fully to half hardy.

CULTIVATION
Grow in fertile, humus-rich, moist but well-drained soil in full sun or partial shade. Can seed themselves to death, so dead-head regularly. V.cornuta will need to be cut back after flowering to keep plants compact and tidy.

PROPAGATION
Violas are easy from seed sown fresh or in spring in a cold frame. Pansies (V.x wittrochiana) can be sown in late winter for early spring and summer flowering, or in summer for winter flowering. Many Violas are short-lived so propagate regularly.

V.'Black Ace' is a startling deepest purple with an orange eye. The flowers are 1.5cm across. (Morris May).
V.'Black from Black' has flowers with thick, rounded intense black petals from March to July and later. A strong grower with a good fruity scent. 15cm. (6").
V.'Black Magic' from the U.S. is a superb viola in containers, midnight black with a yellow eye. 20-25cm (8-10cm) and capable of trailing beautifully.
V.'Bowles Black' (synonym V.nigra) is actually a tricolor Viola with an orange eye and near black flowers. Easy from seed and a favourite with me for its cheeky face.
V.cornuta 'Painted Black' bears near-black flowers.
V.'Midnight Turk' bears delicate, flying, butterfly-like dark purple -black flowers

fromMay to October, mildly spreading. (Bob Brown).

V.'Molly Sanderson' is a sexy black number with the darkest matt black petals with a yellow eye. Low habit and very compact.

V.riviniana 'Purpurea' (synonym V.labradorica h) bears dark purplish green leaves and paler flowers. Can be invasive, but is suitable for the wild or woodland garden in deep or partial shade. 10-20cm (4-8").

V.'Roscastle Black' holds near black flowers well above the foliage from April to July and later. 20cm (8").

V.'Sawyers' Black' is similar to 'Bowles Black' bearing small, velvety purple-black flowers with a yellow eye. 15cm (6").

V.x wittrochiana 'Black' bears silky black blooms with a yellow eye. Some seed catalogues have selected strains of this, which can be found under various names with black in them. Some such as **'Black Prince'** and **'Black Devil'** display large flowers, but I am not convinced that there is much difference between some of these. There are also quite a few f1 strains such as **'Black Beauty'**, **'Black Star'** and **'Clear Crystals Black'**, **'Springtime Black'** and the f2 **'Black Princess'**. 20cm (8").

V.x wittrochiana Swiss Giants Group black bears coal-black blooms. 20cm (8").

WISTERIA

Showy pendent racemes of fragrant pea-like flowers on these climbers and there is one of interest to 'black' flower lovers, but it is not as dark as its synonym suggests. Fully hardy.

CULTIVATION
Grow in fertile, moist but well-drained soil in full sun or partial shade. If grown into a tree, they will need no training, otherwise train against a wall, over an arch or pergola or as a free standing half-standard. Stems twine anti-clockwise.

PROPAGATION
Species can be grown from seed but take many years to flower. Take basal cuttings from sideshoots in early to midsummer and root with bottom heat. Layer in autumn or graft in winter.

W.x formosa 'Kokuryu' (synonym 'Black Dragon' and sometimes wrongly named 'Royal Purple' which is a floribunda cultivar or even wrongly named 'Violacea Plena' which is a brachybotrys cultivar). The real 'Kokuryu' bears deep purple-violet flowers, hanging in racemes. There is a double form, which should also be found called 'Kokuryu' double, bearing fully double flowers of the same shade.

VITIS

The ornamental form **V.vinifera 'Purpurea'** bears attractive leaves, greyish at first , turning plum-purple then deep purple at maturity. The fruits are unpalatable. A hardy, woody deciduous climber which can be used to good effect in the garden.

XANTHORHIZA

Offering bronze to red-purple foliage, this is an interesting choice for moist woodland. Fully hardy.

CULTIVATION
Grow in moist but not waterlogged soil in full or partial shade.

PROPAGATION
Sow seed in containers in an open frame in autumn. Seed is not usually available in the U.K., but is obtainable in the U.S. Divide in spring or autumn.

X.simplissima is a relatively rare thicket forming shrub, which deserves to be more widely available. Yellowroot has erect shoots and bright green leaves to 30cm (12") long, bronze at first then turning red-purple in autumn. In spring, white flowers are borne in pendent racemes as the leaves emerge. 60cm (24") has a spread of 1.5m.

XANTHOSOMA

Blue taro has attractive arrow-shaped, pale purple leaves on deeper purple stems. Frost tender.

CULTIVATION
Under glass, needs a free root run. Loam-based compost with added leaf mould in moderate light, water freely, applying a balanced feed every two weeks. Reduce watering in winter. Outdoors, grow in slightly acid, leafy soil which is humus-rich and fertile in partial shade.

PROPAGATION
Separate tubers at any time of the year.

X.violaceum intermittently bears pale yellow flowers around spadices which are often violet and bears purple stems and leaves. Edible tubers are pink inside. 2.5m.

ZANTEDESCHIA

Another excellent choice for moist soils, both leaves and flowers are attractive. Fully hardy to frost tender.

CULTIVATION
Under glass, grow in loam-based compost in full light. Water freely and apply a balanced liquid feed every two weeks until the flowers have faded. Keep just moist in winter. Outdoors, grow in humus-rich, moist soil in full sun. In frost prone areas, protect Z.aethiopica with a deep winter mulch or grow as a marginal aquatic.

PROPAGATION
Sow seed under glass when ripe. Divide in spring.

Z.'Black-Eyed Beauty' is an elliottiana hybrid with green leaves, heavily white-spotted. In summer it produces cream spathes each with a black central mark in the throat. 30-40cm (12-16").

Z.'Black Magic' is another elliottiana hybrid with heavily white mottled green leaves , bearing yellow spathes , with black throats in summer. 75cm (30").

Z.'Black Forest' is a deep claret-red Arum lily, and deserves to have the word black in its name far more than the other two mentioned here. It has a black inner throat almost forming a stripe to the tip of the flower. Use it as a container plant or cut flower. Bred in Holland and plants are available exclusively through Thompson & Morgan.

ALSO DARK

You may wish to consider some of the following flowers or foliage for inclusion in the dark garden.

Acanthus spinosus forms dark spires.
Achillea 'McVities' is another addition for the chocolate lovers garden.
Agapanthus can be quite dark too and are well worth including, A.'Kingston Blue' bears royal blue flowers. A. 'Purple Cloud' is also dark. Agapanthus inapertus 'Graskop' has blue-black flowers.
Alternanthera are frost tender plants with attractively coloured leaves including purple and bronze.
Apios americana bears clusters of scented chocolate-maroon pea-like blooms.
Artocarpus heterophyllus 'Black Gold' is a variety of Jackfruit bearing large edible fruits with leaves so dark as to appear black.
Other Asclepiads such as Carallumas.
Astelia fragrans has pale silvery brown leaves.
The Astrantias are becoming darker in flower, A.major 'Ruby Wedding' or A.'Hadspen Blood' probably being the darkest on offer, try to see in bloom.
Bartsia alpina is a distinctive and sought after rarity. The flowers, calyx and some of the upper leaves are suffused with a rich dark but somewhat subdued purple.
Bellevalia paradoxa has navy blue flowers which start turquoise-black.
Billbergia amoena comes in varying shades of purple or red flushing.
Many Cactus species bear black spines.
Calceolaria arachnoidea bears rosettes of lance-shaped white, hairy leaves from which arise slender stems of deep purple flowers from summer to autumn. Superb, but probably best in an alpine house.
Cerinthe major 'Purpurascens' borderline dark, but extremely beautiful so perhaps permissible in the dark garden. Navy blue flowers with hints of purple and grey.
Cirsium rivulare 'Atropurpureum'.
Chondropetalum, I only found one reference to this South African grass, resembling Carex and bearing tiny flowers in chaffy brown bracts.
Clematis hybrids, though not as dark as the ones in the main text, you could try 'Etoile Violette', 'Niobe' which I grew some years ago and is a favourite with me for its dark flowers or 'Perle d'Azur'.
Dracaena fragrans 'Compacta Purpurea' bears leaves flushed purple and makes a good houseplant. Mine is quite dark and has attractive, glossy leaves.
Epipactis gigantea 'Serpentine Night' bears purple tinted foliage.
Erica cinerea 'Velvet Night' bears blackish-purple flowers.
Erigeron 'Schwarzes Meer' you may find is darker than 'Dunkelste Aller', but they are not dark enough for my vision of the dark garden. I have seen a description of E.'Quakeress' as having quaker-grey flowers, but it is the foliage which is grey-green, the flowers are a flushed out pink.
Euphorbia characias 'Purple and Gold' has foliage flushed purple in winter.
Ferraria crispa bears few malodorous brown flowers.
Fumaria occidentalis is a rare British native found only in a couple of spots in Cornwall and the Isles of Scilly. It has essentially white flowers which age to red or pink with blackish-red wings of the upper petals and the flowers bordered with white edging.
The deep reddy-browns of the Heleniums may make them suitable candidates.
Helicodiceros muscivorus (Dracunculus) bears maroon-spotted, pale brownish green flowers. Tender. (Bob Brown).
Ipomoea batatas 'Blackie' and I.purpurea 'Kniola's Purple-Black' both bear dark

flowers and the former has edible tubers. Iris iberica is a rare beauty producing brown-veined cream or white flowers, the falls more heavily veined and with black patches and brown purple beards.

There is a dark form of Iris lazica.

Jovibarba, similar to Sempervivum are often flushed brown or red.

Juncus ensifolius, blackish flowerheads.

One of my favourite brown-leaved plants is Kalanchoe beharensis.

Knautia macedonica can have maroonish flowers.

Lagenophora pinnatifida produces mats of bronze-green foliage.

Leucadendrons bear exotic looking flowers, 'Safari Sunset' has stems and bracts of deep wine red in winter.

Leycesteria formosa has dark purple bracts surrounding white flowers.

Lobularia 'Violet Queen' is dark violet.

The flowers of Lotus berthelottii are orange-red to scarlet with a blackish centre, contrasting with the grey-silver foliage.

Medicago sativa ssp falcata is sometimes black but can be variable producing flowers of other colours. They occur when sickle medic is crossed with lucerne. Medicago lupulina is known as black medic.

Melianthus major is a tender shrub which produces spike-like racemes of chocolate maroon to deep red flowers.

Mucuna pruriens can have blackish flowers.

Muscari latifolium bears blackish-violet to blue flowers, the upper petals being paler. M.macrocarpum opens from purplish brown buds to strongly fragrant yellow flowers.

Omphalogramma brachysiphon has black-purple bells whilst O.farreri bears deep purple flowers.

Orchids, many of which are deliciously dark, so I shall choose just a few - Cymbidium 'Mont Millais', Miltonia candida v grandiflora, Paphiopedilum x maudiae, x Wilsonara 'Cheam', x Oda 'Pacific Gold' and the dark Zygopetalums.

Orostachys furusei (Sedum) bears fleshy grey-brown rosettes.

Oryza sativa 'Nigrescens' is an ornamental rice bearing dark brown purple leaves.

Penstemon 'Midnight' for its dark purple-violet flowers, and 'Raven' for its large black-maroon flowers.

Persicaria virginiana 'Filiformis' for its red flushed foliage and small deep red flowers, or P.virginiana 'Painter's Palette' for its dark chevron.

Petasites japonicus v giganteus f purpureus has large rounded leaves which emerge purple-black, maturing to purple-green.

Dark- violet or purple border Phlox - P.paniculata 'Le Mahdi' or try P.x arendsii 'Anja'.

The Proteas offer something of interest too, many having wine-red bracts and P.longifolia is superb with its woolly black centre.

The dark red form of Pulsatilla vulgaris, suitable perhaps if you cannot get hold of the rare P.pratensis ssp nigricans.

If you find dark purples acceptable in flowers, you have a much wider choice including some of the Roscoeas.

Rubus parvus has dark or bronze-green leaves which are paler beneath.

Salvia verticillata 'Purple Rain'.

Scutellaria scordifolia 'Seoul Sapphire' has deep black-purple flushed leaves and indigo flowers.

Tulipa 'Red Riding Hood' has interestingly striped leaves.

Weigela Wine and Roses TM (cv 'Alexandria') was developed in Holland after twenty years of crossing and selection and claims to be the first purple-leaved Weigela. It bears rich, glossy, burgundy foliage and vivid pink flowers. Or try W.florida 'Java Red' - the copper-leaved Weigela.

EMERGING DARK LEAVES

The following is a list of plants whose leaves emerge bronze or purple or are tinted so when young, thereby adding interest and a greater choice for the dark garden. These leaves gradually turn green as the season progresses. Some will hold their colour better than others.

Abelia 'Edward Groucher' has glossy, bronze young foliage.

Acer campestre 'Schwerinii' has purplish emerging leaves which turn purple-green by late summer. A.cissifolium has leaves which open bronze. A.palmatum v heptalobun 'Rubrum' has red young leaves, bronzing in summer with autumn colour of red, orange and yellow.

Adonis amurensis 'Fukujukai' has emerging bronze buds opening to feathery-bronze leaves, later to green.

The dark green leaves of Buxus sinica v insularis are often bronze-tinted.

Catalpa x erubescens 'J.C.Teas' has leaves which unfold purple, those of C.x e.'Purpurea' are dark blackish-purple when young whilst the young foliage of C.bignonioides 'Aurea' is bronze.

Clematis montana v rubens has bronze-purple new shoots.

Corylopsis sinensis v sinensis 'Spring Purple' and C.sinensis v calvescens f veitchiana 'Purple Selection' have purple young growth.

Cotoneaster hummelii bears bronze young foliage, C.insignis bears branches which are reddish-purple when young and also bears blackish-purple fruits.

The young leaves of Diphylleia cymosa are stained red.

Drimys lanceolata bears copper-tinted young growths, with purplish red shoots. Dryopteris erythrosora has bronze, copper red foliage when young.

The shoots and leaf stalks of Emmenopterys henryi are bronze-purple.

Epimedium x versicolor has copper-red and bronze leaves when young as do many other Epimediums.

Euphorbia trigona 'Purpurea' offers young tinted foliage, the leaves dropping at the end of summer. It is a succulent spurge.

Euptelea pleiosperma has young growths which are copper tinted.

Garrya x issaquahensis 'Pat Ballard' is a male form with purple-tinged young foliage maturing to green tinged red, with the additional features of bearing reddish-purple shoots and catkins.

The young leaves of Hamamelis vernalis 'Sandra' are suffused plum-purple, becoming green but still retaining a purple flush on the underside.

Hydrangea serrata 'Preziosa' has purple-tinted leaves when young.

Hypericum offer bronze leaves on H.choisyanum and H.x dummeri 'Peter Dummer', the latter also having a second flush in winter.

The leaves of Idesia polycarpa are purple-tinged when young.

Ilex x altaclerensis cultivars can offer young reddish-purple foliage such as 'Camelliifolia' and 'Moorei'. I.aquifolium 'Donningtonensis' has dark, blackish-purple stems and purple-flushed leaves. I.pedunculosa bears bronze-tinted leaves when young and I.vomitaria is often purple-tinged.

Juglans regia is bronze-purple when young.

Leea coccinea 'Burgundy' is a Burmese shrub producing deep red leaves, the species produces bronzed leaves when young. Make elegant houseplants.

Leucothoe fontanesiana 'Scarletta' has dark red-purple young foliage, turning dark green, with bronze flushing in autumn.

Lonicera nigra has deep purplish shoots,

and the added attraction of green berries which turn purplish black.

Maddenia hypoleuca is an unusual rare shrub or small tree with cherry-like leaves which are bronze-tinged when young and bears small black fruits.

Mahonia aquifolium 'Moseri' has attractive bronze-red young leaves.

Some Malus species have bronzed or bronze-red foliage when young such as M.'Aldenhamensis'.

Nyssa sinensis bear bronze young leaves and provide excellent reddish autumn colour.

Dark blackish purple young leaves are a feature of Osmanthus heterophyllus 'Purpureus'. O.heterophyllus 'Purple Shaft' also has young purple foliage.

Osmunda regalis has coppery-brown leaves as they unfurl in spring. O.r. 'Purpurascens' retains the colouring much better throughout the summer.

Parahebe catarractae has leaves tinged purple when young.

Parthenocissus thomsonii (Cayratia) has foliage which is reddish-purple when young , turning purple-green in summer and finally bright red in autumn.

Another species to offer superbly coloured young growth is Photinia x fraseri. The species offers bronze to bright red foliage. The cultivar 'Birmingham' offers bright purple-red foliage and that of 'Red Robin' is bright red. P.'Redstart' is also bronze-red when young and the species P.villosa makes another good choice for young bronze leaves.

The young growths of Pieris japonica Taiwanensis Group and of P.japonica 'Scarlett O' Hara' are bronze.

Polygonatum 'Betberg' has emerging leaves and stems stained purple.

Populus nigra has dark bark and bronze foliage when young, colours yellow in autumn. P.x canadensis 'Robusta' has bronze-red young leaves in mid-spring.

Many Prunus species and cultivars have bronze leaves when young, such as P.'Kursar' and P.'Pandora'.

Quercus glauca and Q.laurifolia bear bronze young leaves. The young foliage of Q.robur 'Atropurpurea' is red-purple, maturing to grey-purple.

The architectural leaves of Rheum palmatum 'Atrosanguineum' emerge vivid red, the colour being retained better on the underside. R.p. 'Tanguticum' retains its purplish tints even better.

Some Rhododendrons have bronze or reddish-purple foliage when young. R.'Bow Bells', R.'Cowslip', R.'Winsome' and the species R.williansianum are bronze and the new growth of R.'Elizabeth Lockhart' is dark chocolate brown. The Azalea 'Berryrose' has coppery new foliage.

Rodgersia pinnata 'Superba' has mahogany-bronze burnished pinnate leaves when young.

The young foliage of Rosa filipes 'Kiftsgate' is richly copper-tinted, R.longicuspis has dark reddish-brown shoots and copper-tinted young foliage, its white flowers are banana scented. R. x odorata 'Mutabilis' has deep purplish young shoots and coppery young foliage.

Sarcococca 'Purple Stem' has young stems and leaf stalks of a purplish hue.

Staphylea holocarpa v rosea has bronze leaves when young.

The unfolding leaves of Syringa oblata are bronze-tinted but watch late frosts.

Viburnum x bodnantense bears bronzed young foliage and V.carlesii 'Diana' has a distinct purple tinge. V. farreri has bronze young foliage becoming dark green and finally turning to red-purple in autumn. V.tinus 'Purpureum' has leaves tinged purple when young.

LATE PURPLISH OR BRONZE FOLIAGE

The following will provide good autumn or winter colour, ranging from bronze and copper through to deep purple.

Abeliophyllum distichum is a beautiful deciduous shrub related to Forsythia which sometimes turns purple in autumn. Acer oliverianum and A.tataricum ssp ginnala turn purplish-red and offer some of the best autumn tints.

Bothriochloa ischaemum has slender bluish leaves tinged purple in autumn.

Clematis cirrhosa v balearica bears foliage which is bronze-tinged in winter.

Cornus species offer rich purple-red foliage in autumn, choose from C.contoversa which also bears small black fruits or C.kousa 'Satomi', or C.mas.

Corokia 'Frosted Chocolate' bears distinct chocolate coloured foliage in winter.

Cotoneaster can also offer purplish foliage in autumn, amongst the species are C.sherriffii, C.tomentellus and C.villosulus which also offers blackish-purple fruits. C.'Valkenburg' also becomes purplish in autumn.

Cryptomeria japonica 'Bandai-sugi' and C.japonica 'Elegans Compacta' both have dense foliage which turns bronze in winter. Deschampsia cespitosa 'Bronzeschleier' has silvery flower plumes, ages to bronze. Some Ericas are bronzed in autumn such as E.carnea 'Heathwood', E.'Ruby Glow' and E.'Corfe Castle'.

Euonymus fortunei 'Coloratus' bears leaves which are purple throughout winter, particularly when the roots are starved or controlled. E.fortunei 'Dart's Blanket' turns bronze-red in autumn. E.hamiltonianus 'Fiesta' bears leaves blotched with creamy-yellow and pink, turning purple in autumn. It is shy-fruiting. E.oxyphyllus bears leaves turning purple-red in autumn with dark red fruits.

Forsythia x intermedia 'Spectabilis Variegated' bears cream variegated leaves which turn deep maroon and pink in late summer and autumn.

Fraxinus americana 'Autumn Purple' turns reddish-purple in autumn, at other times the leaves are dark green. F.americana 'Rosehill' turns bronze-red, F.angustifolia 'Raywood' can turn plum-purple although they sometimes drop their leaves beforehand, and F.chinensis sometimes gives wine-purple autumn colour. F.nigra merely offers dark brown winter buds.

The glistening green leaves of Galax urceolata become bronze in winter. Lime-free soil.

Hakonechloa macra 'Aureola' has purple stems and the leaves age to a wonderful reddish-brown.

Hamamelis japonica v flavopurpurascens has petals suffused dull red and the calyx is dark purple on the inside.

Hebe 'Blue Clouds' has dark glossy green foliage which is purplish in winter.

Leiophyllum buxifolium is tinted bronze in winter.

The leaves of Leptospermum rupestre turn purple-bronze in very cold weather, its stems are reddish.

Leucothoe fontanesiana bears leaves which turn a rich beetroot-red or bronze-purple especially in exposed positions. The bronze-yellow leaves of L.grayana are tinged purple in autumn.

Some leaves of variants of Libertia ixioides turn orange-brown in winter.

The dark green leaves of Ligustrum obtusifolium are often purplish in autumn, and those of L.'Vicaryi' are bronze-purple in winter.

Another species which offers wonderful autumn colour is Liquidambar. The cultivar offering the darkest foliage colour is L.styraciflua 'Lane Roberts' which has reliable dark blackish-crimson foliage over a long period in autumn, or L.styraciflua 'Burgundy' being dark purple or perhaps L.styraciflua 'Worplesdon' but this does not retain the good purple colour for very long before becoming orange-yellow, L.styraciflua 'Golden Treasure' turns reddish-purple edged with yellow, and L.styraciflua 'Moonbeam' has pale creamy-yellow leaves, turning green and becoming red, yellow and purple in autumn. The leaves of the dense, shrubby L.styraciflua 'Gumball' turn orange-red and purple in winter. The species L.formosana also has purple tints in autumn amongst red and orange.

Some Malus cultivars are bronzed in autumn.

Parrotia is attractively coloured in autumn and is effective as a specimen tree. P.persica turns yellow, orange and red-purple in autumn. There is also a weeping form.

Parthenocissus species offer excellent colour in autumn plus the added bonus of blue or black berries, which can cause mild stomach upsets if ingested. The one I like best is P.tricuspidata 'Veitchii' for its dark-red purple foliage. You could also try P.tricuspidata 'Beverley Brook' tinged purple in summer, but red in autumn, or P.tricuspidata 'Lowii' which is bronzy-red with purplish hints. The species itself is brilliant red to purple and very attractive with deeply 3-lobed leaves.

Persicaria affinis 'Superba' bears rich brown foliage in autumn.

Prunus besseyi has rusty-purple leaves in autumn, those of P.spinosa 'Purpurea' become deep reddish purple.

Pyrus ussuriensis bears foliage which turns bronze-crimson in autumn.

The deeply cut leaves of Quercus ellipsoidalis are quite beautiful in form and turn red-purple in autumn. The foliage of Q.velutina, the black oak, turns red-brown in autumn, the bark is dark brown, almost black hence the common name. Q.coccinea is fabulous in autumn, but probably too red for the purposes of the dark garden.

Rhamnus imeretina bears leaves which are usually bronze-purple in autumn.

The leaves of Rhododendron davuricum 'Hiltingbury' are bronze in cold weather and the pubescent leaves of R.tosaense turn crimson-purple in autumn.

Rhus trichocarpa offers red-purple foliage in autumn, and R.typhina offers purple tints whilst R.aromatica offers foliage which turns orange to red-purple.

Rosa elegantula bears purple and crimson autumn foliage, as does R.nitida and the small, suckering shrub, R.virginiana bears glossy green leaves which turn purple, then orange-red and finally crimson and yellow in autumn.

Shortia has foliage often suffused red in autumn.

Sorbus reducta offers foliage darker than the usual red of most species, turning red and purple. S.scalaris also turns red and purple.

Suaeda vera, a small, native, maritime sub-shrub sometimes turns totally bronze-purple in autumn.

Taxodiums turn rust brown in autumn.

Vaccinium arctostaphylos offers red-brown foliage when young turning to red-purple in autumn with the addition of blue-black berries.

Viburnum x burkwoodii 'Chenaultii' turns bronze in autumn.

The foliage of Zelkova serrata is bronze or red in autumn.

PODS, FRUIT AND BERRIES

The following are interesting for their fruit and berries of purple to black hue. Please do not eat berries or fruit unless you are absolutely sure they are safe.

Many Abies species have violet-blue cones. The seed pods of some Acacia species are tinged red or purple.

Acmena smithii can bear edible red-purple berries, but they can also be white or pink.

Acoelorraphe wrightii bears black fruit.

The berries of Actaea are highly toxic if ingested, A.erythrocarpa bears maroon berries and A.spicata (synonym nigra) bears black berries.

Ailanthus altissima bears red-brown fruit.

Amelanchier species bear spherical or pear-shaped purple to maroon fruits.

Ampelopsis megalophylla bears bunches of black fruit.

Aralia species bear spherical fruits which are usually black as in the case of A.elata and A.spinosa, but dark purple on the species A.racemosa.

Arctostaphylos alpina bears purple-black fruit and that of A.patula is dark brown to black.

Arenga pinnata often dies after fruiting, its fruits are black.

The autumn fruits of Aristotelia chilensis are purple ripening to black.

Aronia melanocarpa, the black chokeberry bears black berries and those of A.x prunifolia are purple-black.

Some Berberis species offer dark fruit such as B.x bristolensis, B.buxifolia, B.calliantha, B.candidula, B.coxii, B.darwinii, B.empetrifolia,B.hypokerina,B.linearifolia, B.x lologensis, B.sanguinea, B.sargentiana, B.x stenophylla, B.verruculosa and many cultivars, the colour varying from purple, blue-black to black.

The long, red fruits of Berchemia racemosa ripen to black, and those of B.scandens are blue-black.

The fruits of Billardiera longiflora are usually deep purple-blue.

Callitris oblonga bears shiny black female cones.

The fruits of Carissa can vary from red to purple-black.

The edible sweet fruits of Celtis species ripen to varying shades of purple and black. C.sinensis ripens to red- brown.

Cestrum species such as C.elegans, C.fasciculatum, C.parqui and C.psittacinum all bear dark berries.

Chamaecyparis thyoides has angular female cones which are purple-black to red-brown.

The small, spherical or ovoid fruits of some Chamaedorea species are black.

Chionanthus retusus species bear blue-purple or blue-black fruits.

Cinnamomum camphora bears black berries.

The dry, unpalatable berries of Cissus antartica are black, those of C.striata are glossy black and those of C.hypoglauca and C.rhombifolia are blue-black.

The red fruit of Cleyera japonica ripens to black.

Clintonia uniflora bears blue-black berries.

Coriaria terminalis has fleshy, dark blackish-red fruit to 1cm across.

Cornus alternifolia, C.contoversa and C.macrophylla all bear blue-black fruit and that of C.sanguinea is dull blue-black.

Corokia buddlejoides bears bright red-black fruit.

Cotoneaster affinis bears dark purple-black fruits.

Daphne bholua bears fleshy, spherical blackish-purple fruit. D.caucasica mainly bears black fruit although the colour can vary and D.laureola and D.pontica both bear black fruit.

Decaisnea fargesii bears unusual and highly decorative pendent, dull blue fruit to 10cm (4") long in autumn.

Dictyosperma album bears purplish-black fruit.

Disporum cantoniense and D.flavens bear dark black or blackish berries.

The midribs of the leaves of Dryopteris wallichiana are covered with dark brown or black scales.

Eleutherococcus species bear black or purple-black fruits.

Empetrum nigrum has black berries, E.purpureum reddish-purple.

Eurya emarginata and E.japonica bear purple-black and black berries respectively.

Fatsia japonica bears spherical black fruit.

Forestiera neomexicana, the desert olive, bears black egg-shaped fruits.

Fraxinus excelsior bears conspicuous black buds in winter.

Fuchsias usually bear purple fruits which are edible, but they do not really taste that pleasant to my palette.

Gaultheria forrestii, G.myrsinoides, G.nummularoides and G.pyroloides all bear dark blackish fuits.

Gaylussacia baccata, the black huckleberry bears edible glossy black fruit.

Hakeas bear warty dark brown seed pods.

Mature Hederas can bear black fruit.

Holboellias irregularly bear sausage-shaped purple fruits.

Hovenia dulcis bears spherical black fruit.

Ilex have male and female flowers borne on separate plants, both are needed to produce berries. I.crenata cultivars such as 'Convexa', 'Golden Gem' and Mariesii' and the form f. latifolia often bear black berries.

Juniperus species bear bluish black fruits.

Lardizabala bear edible sausage-shaped purple berries 5-8cm (2-3") long.

The female cones of Larix are usually purple.

Leycesteria formosa bears red-purple berries.

Ligustrum species can bear blue-black to black fruits.

Some Livistona species bear brownish red to black fruit.

Lonicera giraldii, L.henryi, L.involucrata, L.japonica, L.ledebourii, and L.nitida all bear blue-black, purple-black or black berries, those of L.pileata are violet-purple.

Lophomyrtus bullata and L.x ralphii bear deep black-red berries.

Luma apiculata bears purple berries and those of L.chequen are black.

Mahonia species bear mostly purple to black berries.

Manglietia insignis sometimes bear purple fruit.

Melicytus bear purple berries.

Meliosma have dark fruits of varying hues from red through violet to black.

Menispermum bear grape-like glossy black fruit on female plants.

Morus nigra, the black mulberry, bears edible red fruits turning dark purple in late summer.

Some Myoporum spp bear purple berries.

Myrtus communis bears purple-black berries.

The most interesting black pods are to be found on Nicandra physalodes.

Ochna species can bear lustrous purplish to black fruits contrasting with the thickened and enlarged calyces and receptacles.

The immature green fruits of Olea, the olive, ripen to black.

Ophiopogon species bear blue-black berries, which persist well into winter.

Many Osmanthus species bear blue-black or dark purple fruit.

Osteomeles species bear red-brown, blue-black to black fruits.

Paris quadrifolia bears blue-black, spherical berry-like capsules to 1cm across.

The inconspicuous flowers of Parthenocissus species produced in summer, may be followed by dark blue or black berries.

Pavetta capensis bears glossy black fruits.

Peltophorum pterocarpum bears winged

purple-brown seed pods.

Phillyrea species bear blue-black fruits.

Some Phoenix species bear edible brown or black fruits, including the date palm.

Some female cones of Phyllocladus can be black. Purple male cones are catkin-like.

Phytolacca species bear dark red to purple-black fruits. They can be highly toxic as in P.americana.

Polygonatum species often bear black fruits.

Polyscias species usually bear small purple to black berries.

Some Prunus species such as P.x cistena bear dark purple fruits, whilst P.serotina, the black cherry, bears edible red fruit which ripens to black.

Pseudopanax species bear purple-black to black fruits.

Rhamnus species bear berries which ripen to black.

Rhodotypos scandens bears black fruits.

Rhoicissus species bear tiny flowers followed by red to purple berries.

Some Ribes species bear black fruits or red berries which ripen to black.

Robinias, unless sterile, usually bear dark brown seed pods.

The hips of Rosa pimpinellifolia are purplish-black.

Rubus species often bear black fruits including the edible blackberries and the unpalatable berries of R.cockburniana.

Rumex species bear brown to red-brown fruit.

Salix gracilistyla 'Melanostachys' is distinguished by its beautiful black catkins with red anthers that turn bright yellow.

Sambucus nigra bears glossy red fruit whilst S.canadensis bears spherical purple-black fruit.

Sarcococca species bear dark berries from blue-black or purple to black.

Schefflera species often bear spherical black or blue-black fruits.

Sinofranchetia chinensis bears grape-like purple berries.

Solanum jasminoides bears ovoid black fruit. Aubergine (eggplant) and peppers also belong to this genus and provide dark edible fruits.

If pollinated, Stauntonia bear edible purple fruit to 5cm (2").

Symphoricarpos orbiculatus bears dark purple-red fruit which can cause a mild stomach upset if ingested and contact may irritate the skin.

Syzigium aromaticum (Eugenia), the clove, bears ellipsoid purple fruit.

Tetrapanax papyrifer , the rice-paper plant, bears clusters of black fruit.

Tetrastigma voinierianum bears small, acidic, grape-like, black berries.

The seed pods of Thevetia peruviana are black, each contains one or two highly toxic nut-like seeds.

The male cones of Thujopsis dolobrata are dark violet.

The spherical or kidney-shaped fruits borne on female plants of Trachycarpus are blue-black.

Trapa, the water chestnut bears spiny, hard black fruits.

Vaccinium includes the blueberries and bilberries which are grown primarily for their fruits.

Viburnum x bodnantense is virtually sterile, when it does produce any fruit you can expect it to be blue-black or purple. More reliable for berries are V.cinnamomifolium, V.grandiflorum, V.propinquum and V.tinus which all bear blue-purple-black fruit. V. harryanum, V.foetens, V.lantana and V.odoratissimum all produce red fruits which ripen to black.

Vitis amurensis bears unpalatable, white-bloomed black grapes. V.'Brant' produces large bunches of edible blue-black grapes, V.'Black Hamburgh' is considered one of the best black eating grapes. The ornamental V.vinifera 'Purpurea' bears unpalatable purple grapes.

Some ornamental species of Zea mays produce black cobs.

DARK BARK OR STEMS

BARK

Some Acer species.

Betula nigra.

The trunks or stems of tree ferns are often blackish, such as Cyathea medullaris or Dicksonia squarrosa.

Dacrydium cupressinum has dark brown bark which flakes.

Fraxinus nigra.

Juglans nigra.

Quercus nigra.

Quercus velutina.

Xanthorrhoea known as Blackboy.

STEMS AND SHOOTS

Acer negundo v violaceum bears purple maroon young shoots.

Some Astilbes such as A.x crispa 'Perkeo' have bronze stems.

Baptisia australis bears black swollen seedpods on dark, upright stems.

Colchicum speciosum 'Atrorubens' has purple stained stems.

Cornus alba 'Kesselringii' provides colour in winter with its brownish black stems whilst those of C.stolonifera 'Kelsey's Dwarf' are purplish red.

Daphne longilobata bears purplish stems.

Drimys lanceolata has purplish red shoots.

Some ferns such as Adiantum pedatum bear wiry, brown or black stems.

Eriogonum crocatum has almost black stems.

Hebe decumbens has purplish black shoots, whilst H.ochracea and H.'Carl Teschner' have blackish main stems, and the stems on H.'Mrs Winder' are reddish brown.

Heliconia bihai 'Purple Throat' has maroon stems.

Helionopsis orientalis bears dark red stems.

The fronds of Hemionitis are usally borne on shining black stalks.

Hydrangea nigra has striking black stems.

Ilex x altaclerensis 'Hodginsii' is a male bearing dark purple stems. Other hollies can be found with the same attraction.

Lachenalia species sometimes have mottled stems, marked with purple or brown.

Ligularia 'The Rocket' and L.przewalskii have almost black stems.

Lychnis x arkwrightii 'Vesuvius' has dark stems.

The stems and leaf veins of Pachyphragma macrophyllum are purple tinted in winter.

The stems of Penstemon digitalis 'Husker Red' are beetroot red.

Some Philadelphus.

Phlomis tuberosa 'Amazone' bears dark purple branching stems.

Phyllostachys nigra, the black-stemmed bamboo.

Pilosella aurantiaca has black hairy stems.

Some Salix species bear dark or even purple stems as in the case of S.hastata 'Wehrhahnii', those of S.acutifolia 'Blue Streak' are blackish-purple, covered with a vivid, blue-white bloom. S.daphnoides has white-bloomed, purple-violet shoots.

Schefflera elegantissima has dark blackish stems.

Stachyurus species bear red-brown shoots.

Tamarix tetandra has purple-brown shoots.

Tetrastigma voinierianum has red-brown stems.

Trapa, the water chestnut produces red stalks.

Veltheimia bracteata has yellow-spotted purple stems.

The flowers of Edgeworthia gardneri turn black when dried.

DARK ON THE UNDERSIDE

Often leaves are only dark, usually purplish on the underside. These usually provide a perfect contrast to the surface colour of the leaves and are still visible, particularly when the leaves are unfolding, or when the plant is suitable for a hanging basket.

The leaves of Calathea are attractively patterned on the surfaces and coloured, usually red or purple on the undersides.

Ctenanthe are frost tender plants which can be grown in a shady border in the tropics, but here in the U.K. are best as houseplants. They are related to Marantas and have attractively marked leaves on the surface. C.burle-marxii has deep purple leaves on the underside, those of C.oppenheimiana are wine-red and C. 'Greystar' is spectacular, the foliage purple beneath.

Dioscorea discolor - purple underneath.

The foliage of Hebe 'Ettrick Shepherd' and H.'Midsummer Beauty' is purple on the underside.

Hedychium greenei has maroon on the reverse of its leaves and stems are maroon.

Hoheria populnea 'Foliis Purpureis' bears leaves of plum-purple on the undersides whilst H.'Purpurea' has coppery undersides and H.'Osbornei' purplish.

The pale silvery leaves of Ledebouria socialis are purple on the underside.

Pseudowintera colorata bears pale yellow-green leaves above , flushed pink underneath, edged and blotchedwith dark crimson-purple. The dark red to black fruits are rarely produced in the U.K.

Rheum palmatum 'Atrosanguineum' reddish on the underside.

The leaves of Rhododendron forrestii are purple beneath and those of R.tephropeplum are plum-purple.

The leaves of Rosa longicuspis v sinowilsonii, a climber with reddish-brown stems are purple-flushed on the undersides.

Ruellia devosiana has spreading purplish branches and leaves are purple on the underside only.

Streptocarpus wendlandii is a curious, unusual species bearing one solitary, enormous leaf which is dark purple-green on the surface and red-purple below.

Strobilanthes dyeriana has leaves beautifully marked on the surface and purple beneath.

Stromanthe 'Stripestar' is dark purple on the underside, which is very prominent as the leaves unfurl.

Tradescantia spathacea is a clump-forming perennial with fleshy leaves which are deep purple underneath.

Viola walteri has purple leaves on the underside.

DARK-CENTRED FLOWERS

Most flowers of the daisy family offer black centres and there are a few others having black or purple centres, eyes or blotches.

Allium nigrum bears large heads of white flowers with black middles. Easy. 40cm.

Anemone x fulgens has scarlet flowers with a dark centre, A.pavonina bears solitary flowers with dark centres.

Arctotis 'Zulu Prince' is a favourite with me for its silvery foliage, creamy flowerheads and dark disc.

Some Calochortus are blotched such as C.luteus with its yellow flower, marked maroon, others have maroonish markings at the base of the petals.

Catananche caerulea 'Bicolor' has white flowers with purple centres.

Some white-flowered Cistus are marked with crimson such as C.x cyprius.

Clematis florida 'Sieboldii' bears single white flowers and large bosses of purple stamens.

Clianthus formosus has black blotches on a scarlet flower.

Codonanthe gracilis has maroon spotted white flowers.

Codonopsis lanceolata bears twining, purple-tinged stems and pendent, bell-shaped mauve-flushed, greenish-white flowers beautifully veined with violet.

Delphinium 'Sandpiper' bears semi-double white flowers with brown eyes.

Dianthus 'Alice' is a modern pink with ivory white flowers with a large crimson eye, D.'Forest Treasure' is a border Carnation with double white flowers flecked red-purple.

Dietes bicolor bears small brown marks on the yellowish petals.

Dimorphotheca pluvialis bears whitish flowers with a central dark brown disc, D. pluvialis 'Tetra Pole Star' has pure white flowers with deep violet blue central discs.

Geranium ocelatum and G.psilostemon has brilliant magenta flowers with a black eye, the foliage colours well in autumn.

x Halimocistus wintonensis 'Merrist Wood Cream' bears creamy yellow, dark-banded flowers with a yellow centre.

Halimium 'Susan' has bright yellow flowers with bold red-purple centres.

Helianthus debilis 'Italian White' bears pale primrose to yellow petals with a dark black disc floret.

Hemerocallis 'Pandora's Box' bears pale cream flowers with a purple base and a green throat.

Hibiscus calyphyllus, yellow with an astonishing purple-brown eye, H.syriacus 'Red Heart' with its white flowers and red middle and the lovely H.trionum usually grown as an annual with creamy yellow flowers with a brown centre.

Ixia 'Hubert' bears brownish red flowers and black centres. Other Ixias have dark centres too.

Leptospermum lanigerum bears white flowers with red-brown calyces.

Lilium duchartrei bears white turkscap flowers deeply spotted and flushed purple. Stems are brownish.

Magnolia x weisneri and M.wilsonii, both white with purple anthers/stamens respectively.

Osteopsermum- 'Whirygig' for its unusual petals which almost twist.

Paeonia suffruticosa ssp rockii has white petals with maroon bases.

Ranunculus asiaticus is a pure beauty.

Romulea sabulosa scarlet and black.

Sanvitalia procumbens and Thunbergia alata are orange and black.

Tolpis barbata is yellow with dark maroon.

FAVOURITE BLACK PLANTS

It is difficult to choose favourites when one loves plants so much and especially black ones , but some plants stand out for the intensity of their colour, their valuable foliage or their beauty. I have split them into two separate groups of foliage and flowers. These are my must-haves, the ones I would really rather not be without.

FLOWERS

Arisaema serratum for its incredible beauty. The spathe and spadix is absolutely breathtaking.

Fritillaria camschatcensis for its unbelievably black flowers. Possibly the blackest of all flowers.

Iris chrysographes 'Black Knight' for its deep black colour. A very attractive flower.

Arum palaestinum which is adorable.

Primula auricula, very difficult to choose a firm favourite, I love all of these, not just the dark ones. Perhaps the old cultivar 'Mikado' would be my special choice.

Dianthus barbatus 'Sooty' which I value for that rare combination of dark flowers and especially later in the year, dark foliage.

Tulipa 'Queen of Night' for its dark flowers of beautiful form.

Alcea rosea 'Black Beauty' for its deep nearest to black large flowers.

Aquilegia 'William Guiness' for its delightful black and white blooms. I prefer the single to the double form.

Scabiosa 'Chile Black' (Satchmo) for its dark black buds and its lovely maroon-black flowers.

I could choose more, but I shall end up by repeating all the plants selected for the main text of the book.

FOLIAGE

Ophiopogon planiscapus 'Nigrescens' for its black foliage, a most unusual plant which I would never want to be without.

Fagus sylvatica 'Riversii' I love the purple beeches, and this is a good form with deep colour.

Sambucus nigra 'Black Beauty', perhaps last year my choice would still have been 'Guincho' or even 'Thundercloud', but this new introduction is of an even darker colour and has a pleasant scent.

Colocasia esculenta 'Black Magic' is a firm favourite for its dark stems and its arrow-shaped leaves.

Acer palmatum 'Faassen's Black' difficult to choose just one Acer, I would love to grow them all, for the colour and shape of their foliage, whether they be dark or not.

Sedum 'Lynda et Rodney', last year I would probably have chosen 'Bertram Anderson' which although lax has become a favourite, but the colour and form of 'Lynda et Rodney' seems much better.

Euphorbia dulcis 'Chameleon' is a favourite of mine for the colour of the foliage. Watch the sap.

Geranium pratense 'Purple Haze', again so difficult to choose just one, but this is a favourite for the deep coloured-foliage and the flowers too.

Heuchera I think my favourite of the moment is 'Rachel', but I like to select the different hues of the foliage for different planting schemes, look closely at the leaves, Heucheras are so beautifully and interestingly veined.

Cercis canadensis 'Forest Pansy' I love for the heart-shaped leaves which become so dark.

VEGETABLES AND HERBS

VEGETABLES

Dark leaves and fruits are not confined to flowers. Vegetables offer their fair share of dark beauties some of which will look just as good as anything else in the borders. I have included some roots, whose colour of course, will be hidden until pulled.

ASPARAGUS
'Purple Jumbo' is a unique triploid form offering purple spears above ground which almost appear black during low temperatures. The tender spikes turn to green after cooking. You can use the purple water to make soup, but I always think the delicate flavour of Asparagus is best enjoyed when the spears have been steamed.

AUBERGINE
Known as eggplant in the US, there are some wonderful shiny dark beauties on offer and purple ones too.
'Mini Bambino' is excellent for the small garden, bearing dwarf 2.5cm (1") fruits which can be eaten whole.
'Black Beauty' was introduced in 1910 and its purple-black fruits are still popular today.
'Black Enorma' must be one of the darkest available, it is early and prolific with shiny black fruits.

BEANS
'Purple Teepee' is a French bean which bears stringless pods which turn green on cooking.
'Royalty Purple Podded' is similar.

BEET
Beets can be grown in the border and their ornamental value will enhance any planting with their deep red leaves.
'Bull's Blood' has dark red foliage and 'McGregor's Favourite' offers brilliant blood-red foliage, whilst 'Vulcan' has brilliant red foliage, all can be picked and eaten when young.

BEETROOT
Early beetroot can be sown from April, bolt-resistant varieties from March.
'Boltardy' has a sweet fresh flavour.
'Red Ace' is one of the best for colour as it is almost ring free.
'Rubidus' is perhaps an improvement on 'Boltardy', virtually bolt-free and ready to harvest a week earlier.

BROCOLI
There are early and late purple sprouting varieties, and one of the earliest varieties is 'Rudolph' which produces tasty large spears from January onwards, from mid-February in colder climates.

BRUSSELS SPROUTS
'Falstaff' and 'Rubine' bear red buttons and foliage. The sprouts turn green on cooking.

CABBAGE
There are numerous red cabbages to choose. 'Red Jewel' has large, tightly packed hearts with crisp, ruby-red leaves. Excellent standing quality and good storing ability. Delicious as a pickle or as a lightly cooked vegetable.

CAULIFLOWER
Purple heads against mid-green leaves.
'Violet Queen' bears heads of deep violet up to 15cm (6") diameter. Turns green when cooked.

CELERY
'Giant Red' is a splendid variety with very solid, dark red heads which stand well.

KALE

'Red Bor' with its crinkly purple leaves is highly decorative. It has excellent cold tolerance and crops during autumn to winter.

KOHL RABI

'Blusta' is promoted by T&M as one of the best in recent trials. Purple-blue roots have a resistance to becoming woody with age and a sweet, nutty flavour.

'Purple Vienna' is fast disappearing from seed catalogues and being replaced by new varieties, but I still like it. One of my favourite vegetables and easy to grow.

LETTUCE

Lettuce come in shades from red to purple as well as the usual green.

A new lettuce being trialled at the time of writing by T&M bears claret crinked leaves with a sweet flavour.

'Lollo Rosso' is widely available, with frilled reddish brown leaves but rather bitter I find.

'New Red Fire' is a dark red leaved variety with good flavour.

ONION

The bunching or spring onion 'Santa Clause' has deep red colouring towards the base which is improved by earthing up and the onset of colder weather.

'Red Baron' has dark red skins and its flesh is paler being almost white in the centre.

ORIENTAL GREENS

Hon tsai tai is a flowering purple Pak Choi, both decorative and edible. Mustard Giant Red is also worthy of inclusion.

PEPPER

Such a wealth of peppers to choose from even in chocolate to black colours.

'Sweet Chocolate' has to be a favourite. An early fruiting, cold-tolerant sweet bell pepper which is the colour of plain chocolate. 'Chocolate Beauty' may well be the same thing and in purple there is 'Purple Beauty'.

In hot peppers you may come across 'Pretty in Purple', 'Chocolate', 'Black Dallas', 'Black Cluster' or 'Royal Black'.

POTATO

The darkest are blue.

POPCORN

'Red Strawberry' bears strawberry-shaped deep red cobs which can be popped or used decoratively.

RADICCHIO

Red Chicory has quite a bitter taste, but is good to mix with sweeter leaves. Colouring is good and the red leaves usually have white midribs.

RADISH

'Mantanghong' also known as 'Beauty Heart' has green and white skinned tennis ball sized roots with an inner core of bright magenta.

The winter radish 'Black Spanish Long' has black skin and white flesh and can be eaten raw in salads or cooked like turnip. There is also a round type.

SCORZONERA

This is really black salsify. Easily raised.

TOMATO

Most of the following heirlooms have plum-purple skins.

'Black Crimea', 'Black Krim', 'Black Russian', 'Black Sea Man', 'Brandywine'. You could also try 'Calabash Purple' or 'Prudens Purple'.

WHEAT GRAINS

Some wheat grains to try would be Sorghum or Triticum.

HERBS

Quite a few herbs are available in dark colours. Predominantly Basil, which come in lovely deep purples and can be placed outdoors if only in pots. Angelica, Orach (Atriplex), Sage and Perilla have been included in the main section. Grow on their own in a herb garden or mix in the borders, some are also suitable for hanging baskets. For picking, grow near to the house. Purple herbs look effective grown next to golden foliage.

BASIL (Ocimum basilicum)
Available in diverse leaf shapes and colours, here is a selection of the purple varieties.
'African Blue' is an unusual hybrid between 'Dark Opal' and the camphor basils, it retains the camphor odour which may be offputting, but is attractive for its purplish-blue cast. The variety 'Ararat' has striking foliage infused with purple markings.
'Dark Opal' has red-purple leaves and stems. Try it in basil vinegar. When launched it was extremely dark, but is now producing some green.
Holy basil (o.tenuiflorum syn O.sanctum) is also available in a purple strain.
'Osmin' is perhaps the darkest. 50cm (20"). Purple basil O.basilicum v purpurascens is an annual with strongly scented purple leaves.
'Purple Delight' upright strong growth, and colouring like the old 'Dark Opal' before it became greenish.
'Purple Ruffles' is an annual grown for its attractive ruffled leaves in deep purple. It is not the easiest to grow, damping off easily. Again, it is a strain which is showing some deterioration since it achieved award-winning status. Can be placed outdoors in a sunny position in pots.

'Rubin' leaves nearly pure purple-bronze. Fine flavour and aroma.
'Sian Queen' could be grown for its deep purple inflorescences.

FOENICULUM
Bronze Fennel (F.vulgare 'Purpureum' often sold as Bronze') is highly decorative with bronze-red lacy foliage. There is also a Giant Bronze on the market to further confuse those trying to give plants the correct name.

GRAIN AMARANTH
Amaranthus hypochondriacus included in the main section can be cooked as a hot cereal or popped like popcorn. It can also be milled into flour. Edible landscaping with vibrant burgundy colour.

OREGANO
'Hopley's Purple' bears dark purple green foliage and has a compact growth habit.

RUMEX
Sorrel is another edible landscaping herb, too good just for the herb garden or vegetable patch.
The glossy red leaves of Rumex acetosella ssp vinealis which is particularly good in winter and spring will add interest to the border. Removing flowering tops as they appear will keep leaves tender. Small leaves are delicious.

PURPLE CARROTS
Did you know that orange is not the carrot's true colour?
In the 17th century, carrots were available in purple, white and yellow. The Dutch selected the orange mutant and it became the most popular colour. Trials are currently taking place with 16 new coloured carrots.

PLANTING SUGGESTIONS

PLANTING SUGGESTIONS

Sometimes, especially when plants are new to you, or a different colour to what you normally buy, it is hard to place them in the garden. The following suggestions will be of help.

GENERAL

All dark foliage associates well with silver foliage plants such as Artemisia, Celmisia semicordata, the tender Convolvulus cneorum, Cynara, Pulmonaria saccharata Argentea Group, Salvia argentea, Senecio cineraria or Stachys byzantina. All these plants offer different textures, shapes and patterns and are of great value in the garden.

Black flowers associate particularly well with white counterparts when available and with pale pink flowers or bright dazzling colours of orange, fiery red and yellow. One of the most dramatic colour combinations is deep purple and orange which is simply stunning. You will find in many instances that the dark foliage plants often bear flowers in these colours.

Black plants also associate well with grasses of which there are many purple forms described in the main section, or you could choose a golden grass such as Milium effusum 'Aureum'.

PARTICULAR ASSOCIATIONS

The following are plant associations which I believe work particularly well and you can try them out in your own garden.

Beta 'Bull's Blood' and Senecio cineraria.

Tall Hollyhocks, Alcea rosea 'Black Beauty' associate well with Crambe maritima and Malva moschata f alba.

Snapdragon , Antirrhinum majus 'Black Prince' and Nicotiana 'Only The Lonely'.

Dark-leaved Cannas with brilliant flowers will associate well with the bronzed foliage Crocosmias such as C.'Dusky Maiden'.

Different Solenostemons (Coleus) will give excellent foliage colours from browny-purple, through purple to black, to brilliant red. They look good just on their own. Pinch out well, plant outside when they have reached a decent size and all danger of frost has passed. Do not allow to flower.

Similarly a bed of nothing but mixed dark-leaved Dahlias with their flowers from yellow, through copper to brilliant red would look very good on their own. Mix them with the above and it could look absolutely scintillating.

Achieve good effect by planting Dianthus barbatus 'Sooty' with Rosa rubrifolia and Salvia officinalis Purpurascens Group.

Ophiopogon planiscapus 'Nigrescens' with Galanthus nivalis (Snowdrops) peeping up through the foliage is a lovely sight. A similar effect can be achieved with white or purple Crocus. Ophiopogon also associates particularly well with pink flowers.

Try planting Molinia caerulea purple flowered varieties with a very dark flowered Hemerocallis, a dark foliaged Heuchera and dark Violas or Primulas. This would look good in a large pot. Also in a largish pot you could plant a dwarf purple-leaved Euphorbia, one of the dark Lilies and a dark violet Agastache.

Plantago major 'Rosularis' and Stachys byzantina make a good combination.

Try Papaver 'Black and White' with the darkest Heuchera and silver foliage such as Convolvulus cneorum.

Dark leaved hardy Geraniums (larger varieties not prostrate types) and dark foliage Heucheras associate well with brilliant reds such as Papaver somniferum or you could try P.somniferum 'Chedglow Variegated' which will add further interest to the foliage effect.

Choose a slightly paler pinkish-purple coloured foliage and plant with Tulipa 'Queen of Night' and T. 'Angelique' for a stunning effect, and if you want to bowl them over, chooser darker foliage and contrast it with brilliant reds such as Tulipa 'Abba' or the beautiful fringed T.'Bird of Paradise'.

Violet flowers are enhanced by silvery foliage.

Grow stately spires of dark Delphiniums or Veratrum nigrum and its white counterpart in front of a dark-leaved Cotinus.

Dark-foliage Sedums such as Sedum 'Lynda et Rodney' associate well with the shimmering foliage of Artemisia absinthium 'Lambrook Silver', for added effect add a dark rose behind.

Try Galanthus nivalis (Snowdrops) with Arum maculatum 'Pleddel' or A.dioscoridis v smithii and Helleborus orientalis black.

Astrantia major 'Ruby Wedding' with Aruncus dioicus.

Dianthus 'Black and White Minstrels' form a neat edging to a planting of dark Irises and dark and white Roses.

A dark climbing rose, planted with dark peonies and white peonies in the forefront, and stately dark tall-bearded Iris, edged with dark Dianthus and white Iberis.

Plant moisture loving woodland plants with Rodgersia aesculifolia 'Irish Bronze'.

Rodgersia also associates well with Osmunda regalis and Darmera peltiphyllum.

Enhance the grace of Dierama with much smaller contrasting foliage plants such as silver-leaved Stachys.

Grow a contrasting Clematis through a dark-leaved Cotinus and plant white Madonna lilies (Lilium candidum) in front.

For summer bedding schemes combine tender perennials and annuals, fill in gaps in the borders or create an annual border on its own. Use Dahlias, Cannas, Penstemons, Pelargoniums and annuals such as Solenostemon and Nemophila.

Create carpets of ground cover with Ajuga underplanted with bulbs, or use Ranunculus ficaria cultivars or Trifolium.

GO BLACK
Anything green is out, purple leaves and black flowers are in.
Take down the privet and replace it with a Fagus sylvatica (purple beech) or purple-leaved Prunus hedge.
Exchange Hedera 'Goldheart' for one of the dark ivies.
Choose dark architectural and specimen plants and trees and fill your borders, containers and baskets with your choice of dark plants.
Select black pots, furniture, paint your screens etc. in black or pick out the contrasting colours of red, gold or orange to brighten the scheme. Label plants with black and gold tags.

TROPICAL TOUCH

If red hot and tropical is your taste, dark foliage and flashing, fiery flowers will please. Try Anthuriums, Cannas, Colocasias, Dahlias, Ricinus, purple-leaved Eucomis, Ipomoea, Phormiums and Cordylines, Solenostemon (Coleus - yes they are ideal outside in summer), Codiaeum (Croton), Hibiscus, and black-stemmed tree ferns. The hotter the better. The foliage in a planting such as this will offer every shade of purple to almost black, the black enhanced by the stems of the tree ferns, and flowers will include brilliant and fiery reds, blazing and bronzy yellows as well as hot oranges to enhance the glow. If you can get hold of it Datura metel black will add the finishing touch. The variety in form and size of the lush foliage and the colourful flowers will create a Paradise on earth. All of these tropical plants are tender .

For a smaller planting select your favourites from the above or try Hibiscus 'Coppertone' with Ricinus 'Carmencita', Canna 'Wyoming' and Solenostemon in the foreground.

POOLSIDE PLANTS

The following will create a dark effect by the poolside in constantly damp soil, not water-logged, in full sun.

Astilbe
Darmera
Eupatorium
Gunnera
Helianthus
Hemerocallis
Lysimachia
Persicaria
Rheum
Rodgersia

The following also enjoy moisture retentive soil, offering an excellent choice and endless possibilities for poolside plantings:

Ajuga
Cosmos atrosanguineus
Crocosmia
Euphorbia dulcis
Haloragis
Iris chrysographes
Ligularia
Lobelia from the main section.
Ophiopogon
Osmunda regalis
Plantago
Ranunculus
Sambucus
Trifolium
Zantedeschia

They associate well with some of the grasses, such as Carex pendula, Deschampsia, Miscanthus and Uncinia. To plant in water, try:
Nymphaea
Trapa natans
Zantedeschia

SUMMER BEDDING

Dark plants offer a wide choice for summer bedding displays and my favourites include Solenostemon and Regal Pelargoniums and the remarkable foliage plants such as Phormiums, Cordylines and Ricinus. By choosing contrasting colours and foliage you can achieve a striking display.

Try Ophiopogon planiscapus 'Nigrescens' mixed with the more tender O.jaburan 'White Dragon', with Senecio cineraria 'Silver Dust' behind, contrasting with the spikier foliage of the deep purple Tradescantia pallida 'Purpurea' and the dark blooms and foliage of Dianthus barbatus 'Sooty' contrasting with Nicotiana 'Lime Green' or Nicotiana sylvestris 'Only The Lonely'.

BLACK, PURPLE AND WHITE

This is one of my favourite combinations and can look very classy. Many plants come with black and white on the same flower, such as Nemophila 'Pennie Black', Dianthus Black and White Minstrels Group and Papaver 'Black and White' and these can be incorporated here as well as plants in single colours.

BLACK, PURPLE AND GOLD

A border using this colour combination offers opportunity for dramatic colour contrast. Choose strong golden yellows, vivid purples and the blackest flowers and foliage. Use bulbs in any of the colours to add interest.

This combination is also quite easy to achieve by the waterside. Choose Angelica, Rheum, Rodgersia and Heuchera for dark foliage, and add Ranunculus ficaria 'Brazen Hussy' and Ligularia 'Dark Beauty' with their dark foliage and yellow flowers and Lysichiton americanus for its brilliant yellow flowers and one or two of the yellow as well as black Irises which prefer damp conditions.

BLACK, PURPLE AND RED

An excellent combination already provided by many plants with dark foliage and red flowers such as Lobelia 'Bees Flame', but you can continue the theme by selecting dark foliage and adding vivid red flowers such as Heuchera 'Velvet Night' and Papaver somniferum.

BLACK AND SILVER

This will produce a stunning display, especially if you choose contrasting foliage such as Cynara, Acanthus spinosus, Allium 'Purple Sensation', Ophiopogon planiscapus 'Nigrescens', Cotinus coggygria , a dark Rhododendron, Artemisia, Convolvulus cneorum, Stachys and so on. The silvers will enhance the darker colours.

LONG BORDER

In a long border it is more effective to grade the colouring of the plants and intersperse with silver foliage and the odd gold or red plant. Try placing the black plants either in the centre or at the ends of the border and working your way down through near black, through the purples to lilac, or through the reds to pale pink. Plantings of this kind are best grouped in threes or fives of each plant.

Remember to clothe walls too. Vertical interest is equally important, and do underplant with bulbs.

THE POTAGER

One of my favourite gardening ideas is to mix fruit, vegetables and flowers in the potager. It is quite easy to select dark plants for this kind of garden.

For cut flowers you could choose the black Lathyrus odorota (sweet peas), Rudbeckia 'Green Wizard' or black lilies.

For the arches which flank the paths, choose Vitis, ornamental purple vines or Akebia, Lathyrus (Sweet peas), Rhodochiton, Tropaeolum (Nasturtiums) or beans.

Choose a selection of herbs and vegetables from those mentioned in the book.

A small specimen tree or fruit tree will provide a focal point and you could use purple hedging and dark ivies to adorn the walls.

CONTAINERS

Ideal for many of the tender plants and they can be moved under cover for winter. Combine a Cordyline with a black Regal Pelargonium, a black Viola, a dark Hedera (Ivy), Cosmos atrosanguineus and the contrasting foliage of Senecio cineraria and Helichrysum petiolare.

Black plants can easily be found for any garden situation.

INDEX

For ease of reference, the main section of this book is in alphabetical order.

SUPPLIERS

SEEDS

Ray Brown
Plantworld
St.Marychurch Rd
Newton Abbot
Devon
TQ12 4SE

Thompson & Morgan
Poplar Lane
Ipswich
Suffolk
IP3 3BU

PLANTS

Beeches Nursery
Village Centre
Ashdon
Saffron Walden
Essex
CB10 2HB

Beth Chatto Gardens
Elmstead Market
Colchester. Essex.
CO7 7DB

Burncoose Nurseries
Gwennap
Redruth
Cornwall
TR16 6BJ

C & K Jones
Golden Fields Nursery
Barrow Lane
Tarvin
Chester
CH3 8JF

Cotswold Garden Flowers
Sands Lane
Badsey
Evesham
Worcs.

Dibley's
Llanelidan
Ruthin
LL15 2LG

Fernwood Nursery
Fernwood
Peters Marland
Torrington
Devon
EX38 8QG

Fibrex Nurseries Ltd
Honeybourne Rd
Pebworth
Nr Stratford-upon-Avon
Warks. CV37 8XP.

Field House Alpines
Leake Rd
Gotham
Nottinghamshire
NG11 0JN

Four Seasons
Forncett St.Mary
Norwich
NR16 1JT

Halls of Heddon
Heddon on the Wall
Newcastle upon Tyne
NE15 0JS

Jacques Amand
The Nurseries
145 Clamp Hill
Stanmore
Middx. HA7 3JS

Kelways Ltd
Barrymore Farm
Langport
Somerset
TA10 9EZ

Langthorn's Plantery
Little Canfield
Nr. Dunmow
Essex. CM6 1TD

Manor Nursery
Thaxted Rd
Wimbish
Saffron Walden
Essex. CB10 2UT

Peter Beales
London Rd
Attleborough
Norfolk
NR17 1AY

The Plantsman's Preference
Lynwood
Hopton Rd
Garboldisham
Diss
Norfolk
IP22 2QN

RD Plants
Homelea Farm
Chard Rd
Tytherleigh
Axminster
East Devon
EX13 7BG

Rowden Gardens
Brentnor
Nr.Tavistock
Devon
PL19 0NG

Stillingfleet Lodge Nurseries
Stillingfleet
York. YO19 6HP

Wychwood Waterlilies
Farnham Rd
Odiham. Hook
Hampshire
RG29 1HS

US SUPPLIERS
Websites
www.asiatica.com
www.glasshouseworks.com
www.heronswood.com
www.terranovanurseries
www.waysidegardens.com

Shuo Wang
Hexe Prefecture Imp & Exp Corp.
17 Xing Cai Rd. Hexe City.
Shandong Province
P.R.China PC 27 4012.

ACKNOWLEDGEMENTS

This book would have been impossible if not for all the help I have received from nursery men and women and seed suppliers around the country. They have provided descriptions and photographs for the book which have made it the comprehensive guide that it is. If I have inadvertently missed anyone out, it is not intentional and I hope I shall be forgiven.

First of all I would like to say I owe my most grateful thanks to Ray Brown of PlantWorld, Devon, not only for all his help and time but also for supplying so many of the photographs for the book, and above all for his support in bolstering me up when I was slip-sliding.

My appreciation also goes to John Carter of Rowden Gardens for his help with descriptions of the many Ranunculus ficaria cultivars from the NCCPG and to William Lyall at Manor Nursery for helping with descriptions and for his promotion of my last book, Kevin at Beeches Nursery, for descriptions, Howard Wills of Fernwood Nursery on Sempervivums and to Nancy Heckler in the USA who so willingly gave her time to provide me with descriptions of black plants that are only out in the US and not over here yet, and of others I did not know of, I hope Nancy will find something new to her in this book ,also for directing me to some wonderful websites and for her generous support, I know she shares my enthusiasm.

I am also indebted to the following who provided descriptions of one or two of the species entered in the book -
Andrew Bateman of Mulu Plants, Beth Chatto whose catalogue is as good as a gardening book in itself, Bill McHugh of Skipness Plants, Bleddyn and Sue Wynn-Jones of Crug Farm for directing me to their website, Bob Brown of Cotswold Garden Plants, Collinwood Nurseries, Derek Lloyd Dean, Dibley's, Doug & Vivi Rowland, seed suppliers, Fibrex Nurseries, Gary Dunlop of Ballyrogan Nurseries, Jean & Richard Wiseman at Ravensthorpe Nursery, Jim Cave, Judith Lockey, mail order Manager at Halls of Heddon, Kelways, SM & ND Chandler at The Old Withy Garden Nursery, RD Plants, Richard Ball of Four Seasons, Robin Savill Clematis, Roger Gilbert of Silverdale Fuchsias, Morris May of Planta Vera,Nigel Wright Rhododendrons, T.A.&D.J.Bushen of Halsway Nurseries, Tim Fuller of The Plantsman's Preference.

Thanks also for their lists and catalogues, all of which include plants in this book, to Abbotsbury Subtropical Gardens, Avon Bulbs, Brian & Heather Hiley, Burncoose & Southdown, Camellia Grove Nursery, Chessington Nurseries, Chris Pattison, Cuckoo Mill Nursery, Cutting Edge Nursery,Eastgrove Cottage Garden Nursery, Field House Alpines, Keepers Nursery, Langthorns Plantery, Loder Plants, Millais Nurseries, New Barn Aquatic Nursery, Perry's Plants, Sheila Chapman Clematis, Stillingfleet Lodge Nursery, The Herb Garden,Water Meadow Nursery & Herb Farm,Waterwheel Nursery, Whimble Nursery, William T Dyson, Wychwood Waterlilies, Wye Valley Plants.

Many of the above nurseries are holders of National Collections which are always worth visiting. Ray Brown at Plantworld, John Carter at Rowden Gardens, Howard Wills and Gary Dunlop to name but a few. For further information or to join the NCCPG, please contact them at The Stable Courtyard. Wisley Garden. Woking. Surrey. GU23 6QP.

PHOTO CREDITS

My grateful thanks go to the following
for providing transparencies for the
book. The copyright for each belongs to
the person or company named below.

Howard Wills, Fernwood Nursery -
Sempervivums.
Robin Savill - Clematis.
Tim Fuller, Plantsmans Preference - Fritillaria.
Shuo Wang - Paeonia hybrids.
Jacques Amand - Arisaema griffithii.
Collinwood Nurseries - Chrysanthemum
'Black Magic'.
Richard Bell, Four Seasons Nursery - Iris
hybrids, Heuchera 'Velvet Night',
Hemerocallis 'Purple Rain', Clematis recta
'Purpurea', Eupatorium 'Chocolate'.
Karen Platt - Bromeliads, Purple foliage,
Begonia, Crinum, Colocasia, Heuchera 'Palace
Purple', Lathyrus, Torenia.
Thompson & Morgan - Dianthus 'Black &
White Minstrels', Primula auricula
'Gizabroon', Scabiosa, Nemophila, Basils, Kale
and Lettuce(Photographic Loan Library).

All other photographs - Ray Brown.
Plantworld. Devon. Photographic Loan
Library. Tel: 01803 872939.